Footprints of a Sea Change

Footprints of a Sea Change:

Mapping the Impact of Gulf Migration on Muslims in Kerala

Dr. Ashraf P

Dr. C. Vinodan

KALPAZ

ISBN: 978-93-5324-277-0

First Published, 2020

Published by

Kalpaz Publications
C-30, Satyawati Nagar,
Delhi – 110052
Ph.: 011-47034999, 9811692060
www.kalpazpublications.com
E-mail: kalpaz@hotmail.com

Printed at: G. Print Process, Delhi

Contents

Acknowledgement

This book is based on our indepth research on temporary labor Migration from Kerala to the Gulf countries. We are grateful for a number of friends and colleagues to encourage me to conduct a detailed study on the subject and publish it. First of all, We would like to express our deep and sincere gratitude to the Teachers and colleagues at School of International Relations and Politics, Mahatma Gandhi University Kottayam, they delivered valuable guidance in a helpful way throughout the study.

We duly concede for the help given by our friends. Special thanks to Mr. Faiz Babu, Mr. Sudheep MS. Mrs. Ramsiya, Danish Rehan and Ishan Afrin. Without their support, co-operation and prayer our attempt would not have been accomplished. We are very happy to express our heartfelt thanks to our Colleagues and relatives for their help, encouragement and co-operation throughout in this work. Above all, we bow the God Almighty for managing us through righteous way.

Preface

Seventeen decades ago, an unfold treasure of gold found in California of United States, triggered millions of dreams in the coming years. The gold rush of 1849, in one way or the other, persists even now with migrants crossing the border in each minute. The dunes with oil becks also were of course a source of dream for a few. The dream hunters from Kerala crossed the Arabian Sea to dig out the luck from the oil fields of Persian Gulf and related industries. Setting the big trend of Gulf migration, Muslim community, especially the Muslims in Malabar, discovered dream destinations even in the remotest sides of Arab world, which in turn ended up with regular route both by air and sea. The mass migration to Gulf Countries from Kerala, especially from Malabar, since 1970s has transformed the state into prosperous and financially secure. Otherwise pushed towards the margins in terms of money and power, the Muslims of Kerala rejuvenated themselves through the dream hunt from the Gulf dunes. The Muslim populated regions of Malabar showed a sign of economic and social development as Gulf Migration commenced. The economic prosperity and subsequent progress in the standard of living started reflecting in the socio-political life of the Muslims in Kerala especially in Malabar. But money was not the only thing that migration has brought.

Gulf migration took Muslim community to a different degree of socio-political impact. Muslims constitute 45 percent of the total emigrants in the Gulf from Kerala, although their share in the total population was only about 26 per cent. Of the total remittances from Gulf, Muslim households received 46.5 percent in 2011. While the average emigration rate in the state is 22 per cent, among the Muslims it is as high as 49 percent. According to Pravasi Malayali Census

Report of the Government of Kerala, the six districts from Malabar have 48.62 per cent of the Gulf migrants. In Malappuram district, 71 per cent of the households have in them either an emigrant or returned emigrant each. Other things being equal, migration rates should be higher in areas which the proportion of the Muslims is high. It is clear and obvious that the set of circumstances has undergone a radical change and which is writ large in the way Muslims in Malabar live today.

From investments to infrastructure, from life to religion, from food to fashion, Gulf Migration has intensively influenced Malabar. In fact, Kerala has become a part of Gulf-life, if not geographically and politically, but very much so economically, socially and culturally. What happens in the Gulf States has echoed in every nook and corner of the state; and what happens in Kerala has, in turn, effected in Gulf countries too. The consumer culture of Kerala is largely restructured after 1970s. From Chocolates to Biriyani, the taste buds were redefined. Smaller to Medium enterprises sprouted in Kerala, especially in Malabar. Most of them were even named with Persian Gulf traits. Religious leaders and the institutions were integrated into the changes coupled with people frequenting abroad. The deep-seated Gulf intimacy always influenced the plans, policy and programmes of various religious groups too. They explored a new medium of messages and missionary, and stepped in to the new arena of cultural sphere. The new trends and movements erupted in the Arab Islamic world were fast incorporated into Muslim organizations in the state.

Noticeable lifestyle change has come to pass due to continuous contact with Arab world. The influence is not only in the ideology and modus operandi of the religious organizations but also found in the performing of everyday prayers and rituals. In another means the Gulf relation has been an instrumental for the transformation of popular Islam in to the slow and steady emergence of Scriptual Islam. The successors of *Sufi* ancestry took a new religious road as gulf migration caused ideological influence. Since *Gulf Salafism* spread across the length and breadth of the state, there has been a pointed attempt to relocate the religion from the living premises to closed-room spiritual routines. The phenomenon widely known as *Neo Salafism* sent shockwaves across the sphere of plural culture prevalent in the state. Focused fully on religious rituals, *Neo Salafism* featured a kind of spiritual extremism.

Gulf migration also has been instrumental in democratization of Muslim society in Kerala. It's no surprise to see that migration to gulf destinations send a wind of democratic change in Muslim community. The quick economic progress in the wake of migration to gulf awakened the people at the bottom of the society. It triggered a remarkable change in the social status of Muslim women too. Hard earned money from the dunes paved the way of education for Muslim community as well. The backward Malabar in terms of the proportion of educational facilities witnessed commencing of countless educational institutions in the early 1990s. The new educational trend set following the exponential growth of academic institutions provided more avenues for girls to experience experiment and explore a wealth of knowledge and excel in academic performance. Thus, women marched to progressive roles in the society. Their freedom of expression and financial self-sufficiency empowered them.

Abbreviation

SKSSF - Samastha Karala Sunni Students Federation
SSF - Sunni Students Federation
SYS - Sunni Yuvajana Sangam
SBV - Sunni Bala Vedi
SKIMVB - Samastha Karala Islam Matha Vidhyabhyasa Board
SKJU - Samastha Karala amiyyathul Ulema
MSM - Mujahis Students Movement
MGM - Mujahid Girls Movement
KNM - Kerala Nadvathul Mujahideen
JIH - Jamathe Islami Hind
SIO - Student Islamic Organisation
GIO - Girls Islamic Organisation
SMF - Sunni Mahallu Federation
KMCC - Kerala Muslim Cultural Centre
MSF - Muslim Students Federation
IUML - Indian Union Muslim League

Glossary

Alim	-	Scholars of Islamic Theology
Bidah	-	Innovation in religious matters
Dars	-	Traditional Arabic Schools attached to mosques where classes are conducted in different tradition in Islam
Fatwa	-	Legal openion of a recognized Muslim jurists or scholar
Hadith	-	Tradition of words and deeds of Prophet Muhammed
Islahi	-	Mujahid movement for reform in Islamic theology
Jaram	-	Tomb of holy persons
Karanavar	-	Head of matrilineal family
Kazhi	-	Leader of Friday prayer in local moques
Kudiyan	-	Tenant
Madrassa	-	Religious School
Mahallu	-	Muslim Village attached to a congregational Mosque
Mullakka	-	Religious teacher in local madrassas
Musliyar	-	Teachers of the local Madrassa
Nercha	-	Offering, vow a religious festival in local mosques for the Honour of Muslim saints
Pardah	-	A Veil worn by Muslim women
Shariah	-	Islamic Theology
Shafi	-	One of the four Sunni schools of Islamic Law
Sheik	-	Spiritual Leader
Taravadu	-	Joint family
Tangal	-	A honorific term applied to a dissidents of Prophet Muhammed a term peculiar to Mappila tangal are religious leaders as well
Ulema	-	Theologians well versed in Islamic Sciences

Chapter - 1

Tracing the Navigation

Along with international flows of capital, information, and technology, Human migration is one of the major forces of change in the world. Approximately 244 million people live outside their country of birth (Mc Aliffe and Martine 2018: 2). The United Nations estimates that, 2.6 million people migrated annually from less-developed to developed countries, seeking employment, reuniting with family, or fleeing conflict and persecution as refugees and internally displaced persons. In most instances, migration is the motivation for a better today and tomorrow. The rapid, repetitive and rising run of people for favorable geographic, economic or professional environment is changing the demographic composition of both receiving and sending societies, and creating new connections between them, with profound implications for social, economic, cultural and political life. Migration is of course, change and it can lead, in turn further transformation both in sending and receiving societies (Portes 2008: 1). As a form of change, international migration is analyzed as a consequence of a diverse set of causes both in the origin and destination countries.

Mass migration culture always shapes up an aspiring attitude among Indians too. Among five distinct streams of international migration, temporary labor is the predominant type of migration found in India, whereby millions of left behind families have remittances from foreign countries for a better living index. Such migration has its own dynamic relation with the social relations. The gulf boom which pulled away people in the beginning of 1970s is a case in a point. The gulf migration always acted upon the various sectors of the society in India. Embarked for Gulf to go back with a pot of gold, the gulf migration has an immense impact on the socio-economic life of people in the country.

Kerala, the Southern state of India, boasts of the bulk of the migrants to Gulf. The Migration to the Persian Gulf from Kerala since 1970s has brought to the state an intense period of prosperity, sense of financial security and social change. Gulf migration and subsequent remittance has changed the entire fate of Kerala society. It has been visible in every facet of social life. Migration thus helped people in Kerala, especially expatriates to put better food on the table. Setting the big trend of Gulf migration, Muslim community, especially the Muslims in Malabar, discovered dream destinations even in the remotest sides of Arab world, which in turn ended up with regular route both by air and sea. The community has been able cash in on every opportunity from the oil-rich land and life of expatriates in the Middle East has since taken a turn for the better. Hence the influence of the migration on the socio-political life of the Muslims in Kerala attracts extra special attention.

The world over, human migration poses serious and significant challenges to governments. Being curious of seeking fair fortune, millions of people all over the world move out of their normal places of residence to new destinations. If military operation, or political oppression or religious prosecution were the major causes of mass departure on various occasions in the past, it is by and large luring economic factors that lead people to migrate in the modern period. Migration gets more and more globalized with cutting-edge communication and transportation technology coming to the fore. Migration is having far reaching impact not only on the migrants but also the society at large both in the place of origin and destination (Joseph 1998: 23).

There are five distinct observable streams of migration in India. In the first place, the indentured labor migration took people mainly to tropical and subtropical lands. It came under fire from many corners only to be abolished by the then government in 1916. In the second place, under Kangani system of recruitment, labors were moved abroad. Labors were recruited first to Sri Lanka, then to Malaya and Burma. The then government in 1938, put to an end to the system. Unbound emigration of traders was the third kind; skilled and semi-skilled workers to East Africa and other parts of the world. The practice went on till the Second World War. Forth category of international migration was that of well educated class or professionals set off to Europe and North Africa. The last and high-flying type of migration took place when thousands of people responded to the exploration of crude oil in Gulf and subsequent developmental activities triggered in those countries (Madhavan 1985: 460).

Among the states and union territories in India, Kerala is at the front of the flight with the highest number of emigrants in west Asia. According to a study conducted by the Centre for Development Studies, the number of emigrants living abroad in 2014 is estimated to be 2.4 million (Zakaria and Rajan 2015:06). Of this, 90% of the total number of the migrants is in the Gulf countries. Gulf migration has so far acted, either directly or indirectly, on the culture, cuisine and cloth of almost all families in Kerala. Migration is affecting every facet of life in Kerala's economic, social, demographic, political and even religious outlook. According to a brief study 21 percent of households have at least one emigrant in Kerala. Geographic distribution by district of origin shows that the largest number of emigrants originated from Malappuram. According to the statistics produced by the Kerala migration Survey, 53.7 percent household have at least one migrant in the same district (Zakaria and Rajan 2015:35).

In 1970s, the backward of district of Malabar in Kerala, had a hand-to-mouth existence due to high unemployment which threw people out of their own land in their struggle for survival. Later the trend hit other districts too. At the crossroads of a big change, modern Kerala took the shape what we see today. Amartya Sen pointed out that during 1970-71 and 1987-88, poverty in the state hit low from 69% to 44%, a massive 25% reduction though there was practically no poverty alleviation action plan in place to the effect; thanks to the regular remittance by expatriates in Gulf. Though we count poverty alleviation and economic prosperity of the state as key advantages, migration to Gulf States has other affirmative aspects too. In fact, Kerala has become a part of Gulf-life, if not geographically and politically, but very much so economically, socially and culturally. What happens in the Gulf States echoes in every nook and corner of the state; and what happens in Kerala has, in turn, effect in Gulf countries too. Even the cultural specialties of the host countries have influenced the behavior and life style of the migrants. Of course, it will also reflect in their social life and political activities.

Muslims, Malabar Muslims in particular, lead the way for destiny-seeking race to the Arab world. Being identified with the big religion of Arab world, the firm relationship between the pioneers and Arab grew from strength to strength. Apparently, Gulf countries seem to be the most favorable career destination of emigrants from Kerala. It's no wonder more members of Muslim community in the state go to Gulf States. Other things being equal, migration rate should be higher among the Muslims or in area in which the proportion of the Muslims is high. (Zachariah, Mathew and Irudayarajan 2003:162). The population movement bore fruit and Muslims in Malabar became one of the major harvesters among the migrant community in the Middle East from Kerala. Migration especially the Gulf migration has so far given new economic strength to the state. It's worth taking note of the fact that almost all the Muslim families in the same area have been connected to Gulf migration in one way or other. It's unquestionably clear and plain that they have made capital out of the migration to Gulf to secure a well-off life back home. This in return made Keralites increasingly conscious about every bit of political development in the region with hope or alarm.

Gulf migration, beyond doubt, played a pivotal part in remodeling, revitalizing and reconditioning the economy of the state of Kerala. It's not confined to the makeover in the sphere of economic prosperity and well being or the change in their life style and food habit. The migration has been on course beyond the social life of the Muslims in Kerala. Concrete buildings put up every nook and corner of Kerala to reflect change in the infrastructural landscape with modern facilities. Quality education became the basic need and norm for expatriates trusted their children with the education and this further enhanced the community's career prospects, social positioning and the political participation. The rising tide of post-migration lifted the community on contrary to the former status of being a backward minority class. Above and beyond all affirmative action accomplished by governments, the progress the migration brought to the state is incredible to date. Migration and money remittances rhythmically pumped loan and logistics to the pace of progress to put a spurt on economic development in the state.

A strong and long tradition of migration is always credited to the south Indian state Kerala. Keralites loved the adventure to travel and put up elsewhere in the world even years before the formation of present Kerala state. Before 1957, the year of Kerala formation, the state's political geography had three parts viz., Travancore, Kochi and Malabar. Among these, people from Malabar, Mappila Muslims constitute very high proportion in labour magration. (Joseph 1998: 42). The 20th century documented two vital streams of migration. The first case scenario was farmers on the road from Travancore to the highlands of Malabar, and the second and most important stream was the migration of semi-skilled and unskilled laborers to the Gulf countries. Existing literature indicate that both these migration streams have induced profound socio-economic changes in Kerala society. Among these two, the Gulf migration is unique and far reaching phenomenon.

Migration to the gulf countries since the 1970s has brought to Kerala an intense period of social change. Every community and even every village has directly or indirectly related to the Gulf migration in one way or other. Muslims, one among the backward communities in the Kerala is the major beneficiaries of Gulf migration as well as Malabar, the most backward region in the state. Gulf migration brought about a sea-change in the social life of the Muslims in the State. Muslims in Malabar until recent decade was socially and economically backward. Gulf migration, which began since the 1970's, had brought about a dramatic change in their social and economic life. More than 70% of the migrants from Malabar region belong to the Muslim community. The migration provided a better economic prosperity to the society. Naturally the economic prosperity led to social development. The economic prosperity and subsequent progress in the standard of living reflect in the socio-political life of the Muslims in Malabar.

Income increased manifold in the migrant-dominated villages. Many poor families came to pass rich and upstarts overnight. Significant growth of 'nouvean riche' upset social hierarchy and rural power structure. Well-to-do position and status enjoyed by a few families only because of ownership of huge wealth and holdings of land were rocked. The process was much visible among Muslims. Sudden surfacing of a new class in the society reflected on everyday social life. Traditionally, a few families of landlords were the leaders of Muslims in rural areas of Malabar. They had a kind of reputation. They had also enjoyed a kind of immunity among community members. Members of the creamy layer were believed to be head and shoulders above the members in the Muslim community. In many cases, they even played an upper hand over religious leadership too. There witnessed a tailspin effect of the convention of might-makes-right following the flood of people to Gulf and turned the environment into a level playing field. It was a big leap in the process of social transformation of Muslims in Malabar.

Religious affairs were put in another order and the structure and pattern of various denominations in the Muslims too. Religious leaders and the institutions were integrated into the changes coupled with people frequenting abroad. The deep-seated Gulf intimacy always influenced the plans, policy and programmes of various religious groups too. They explored a new medium of messages and missionary, and stepped in to the new arena of cultural sphere. The new trends and movements erupted in the Arab Islamic world were fast incorporated into Muslim organizations in the state.

All local religious institutions of the Muslims were under the control of a few fortune-families for years. Exemptions were very a few. Of course, Muslim clerics had their weighty roles, but were very limited. The family members of major 'Tharavadu'(ancestral homes) were in the line of leadership always. They jockeyed for key position of such institutions. Muslims who belonged to the jurisdiction of a specific 'Mahallu Committee' were bound by the committee's final say on matters affecting their private and public life. The traditional landed class could always exercise their power in the name of Mahallu committee. The social position of these people seemed very high in the structure of the society. The social status and power was purely hereditary. Gulf migration presented more rags to riches stories and the hereditary supremacy of the 'Tharavadu' members fell to pieces.

To sum up, Gulf migration has its pivotal role to transform the entire socio-political life of the Muslims in Malabar. It is also tangible in every sphere of their community life too. It will take several more years before the full impact becomes evident. Behavioral changes are slow to come by and usually take a generation or more to become fully visible.

Conclusions drawn applying a fistful of social sciences especially Economics, History, Sociology, Population et cetera, on Gulf migration have different measure of contents and credibility. Much of our understanding of the characteristics and impact of migration in Kerala has always been restricted to economic dimension (Prakash 1978; Mathew and Nair 1978; Sekhar 1993). Bearing this view in mind, this study attempts to discuss the whole gamut of migration over and above the realm of economic advantages and related remittances issue. What's untold is that migration has been affecting every other facets of life in Kerala viz., economic, social, demographic, political, religious et al. Sad to say, economic aspects have been the centerpiece of almost all academic researches on migration so far. However, a few cases of exceptions are found against the trend with a little interest in cultural sphere also. The socio-political dimension of brain drain is still a dark area of research. Hence it is very vital to look at the Gulf influence on the socio-political life of the Migrants.

Gulf migration took Muslim community to a different degree of socio-political impact. The case is demanding special attention because of their participation in the process of moving to Gulf. Muslims constitute 41.3 percent of the total emigrants in the Gulf from Kerala, although their share in the total population was only about 26 per cent (Zachariah and Rajan 2015: 09). Of the total remittances from Gulf, Muslim households received 36.2 percent in 2014. While the average emigration rate in the state is 22%, among the Muslims it is as high as

49%. According to Pravasi Malayali Census Report of the Government of Kerala, the six districts from Malabar has 48.62 %. In Malappuram district, 71 % of the households have in them either an emigrant or returned emigrant each (Zachariah 2007:8). Other things being equal, migration rates should be higher in areas which the proportion of the Muslims is high. These statistics is just enough to establish the significance of the study on Muslims relations to Gulf migration.

The most important phenomenal transformation the migration brought to us, as stated already, is the socio-political influence which has controlled the entire life of the Malabar at least last four decades so far. It is clear and obvious that the set of circumstances has undergone a radical change and which is writ large in the way Muslims in Malabar live today. Such an issue being worthy of great attention, concerning the Muslim psyche and how far it influences the existing social and political scenario in Malabar, is the focal point of the research.

The exchange of views on migration development goes further on than the limited circle of economic development and prosperity in this book. This study takes stock of how migration makes changes to individuals and communities. The focus of the book will be the specific features of the Muslims in Malabar and the changing pattern of their socio-political life. The broad question of this study is to find out how the long term relations and the experience of the migrants with the Arab world significantly influenced the class structure, social hierarchy, worship patterns, and above all, religion and religiosity of the Muslims in Kerala.

Finally, It is a detailed case study illustrating the positive and negative outcomes due to Gulf migration among the Muslims in general and Muslim denominations in particular in Malabar. Keeping the influences the socio-political life of migration in mind, various pieces of information about certain crucial areas have been picked up. The socio-political life of the Muslims in Malabar is studied with the detailed analysis of facts and figures. The attention of the present study is at the three level of the socio-political life of the Muslims in Malabar. The first one is the micro level or individual level, meso level or family level is the second and the macro level or the community level is the third case. At the individual level, the study examines the influence of the Gulf experiences on migrant's social life and political perspective. At the family level, the study tries to find out changes which occur in family circle. It also examines how and what extent the migrants' views and concepts on day today life has influenced his or her family members. The macro level, the study examines how the migration and subsequent remittances altered the existing social power structure within Muslim Society. It is also analyses the transformation of the religious organizations and institutions.

The first and the most important question is whether the gulf connection has influenced the Socio-political life of the Muslims in Kerala, If so, up to what extent? To find out an objective answer for the above said questions, it is necessary to analyze social structure and pattern of the Muslims in the state. So the major problem is how the Gulf migration influenced the local power structure within the Muslim community, especially in the light of the vast changes occurred in the religious institutions and their administrations. The administration of 'Mahallus' and 'Madrassas' (religious schools) are the two important institutions to be examined for this purpose. The proposed study will go in to a detailed analysis on the transformation of the internal power structure of the Muslim community. It is also examines what way the gulf migration questioned the social hierarchy within the Muslim community and the changing pattern of the social stratification.

In this book, my attempt is to investigate whether the constant relationship with the Arab world and the subsequent remittances has influenced the functioning and the methodology of the spread of religious organizations. It also examines the reorientation of Muslim immigrants' lifestyle in Gulf countries and with the newly created wealth, there has brought about any major change in the lives and religious practices of the upstarts, their friends and family members home. Another major question that this study investigates is whether migration–centered religious reorientation of Kerala Muslims are abetting assertion of communal identity, fundamentalism in religious practices, proliferation of radical religious groups and similar things. Another major question of this research is to find out the relation between the migration and women empowerment. The last but not least important question is how far gulf money has so far oiled the wheels of local development and poverty alleviation mission. Another case bound to happen is the media literacy of the Muslims in Kerala and its relations to gulf connection: whether migration has played any role in the internet and social media experience of the Muslims in Kerala. Besides, the study considers supply of gulf money in education sector and changing pattern of Religious education of Muslims.

Chapter Scheme

For better clarity and clarification of the problem, the this book is divided in to seven chapters. The first chapter contains '**Tracing the Navigation**' which I single-handedly followed through my work. It can provide a bird's eye view of the case under study. The second chapter '**Finding the Compass** examines the theoretical aspects of migration and social change. This chapter is again divided in to three subsections. The first subsection deals with different theoretical schools of migration and various definition of the term. It helps to get clear-cut idea of the word migration. In the next subsection under 'Social Change', we examine the definition and the scope of the term 'social change. In the third subsection, the relation between migration and social change is well put. The Third chapter '**Mapping the Footprints**' is a detailed and historical analysis of the Indian Migration to different parts of the world. Kerala's age old contact with the Arab world and the subsequent mass migration to the Persian Gulf is depicted in the fourth chapter '**Bridging the Gulf**. It unveils the historical roots of the gulf migration from Kerala. In this chapter, we examine the characteristics and ups and downs in the Gulf migration.

The fifth chapter **Ups and Down along the Wave** will provide a detailed commentary on the historical roots of the socio-political life of the Muslims in Kerala. This chapter has been divided in to three parts. The first part explores the early history of the Muslims in the state. It stretches from the arrival of Malik Dinar to the beginning of the second half of the 20th century. The second part examines the socio-political life of the Muslims in the post-independence India, but it ends in 1970s, because Gulf boom starts at this juncture. The third part examines the socio-political development which occurred in the Muslim community in Kerala in last three decades.The Sixth chapter '**Sea of Changes**' unveils the impact of the Gulf migration on the socio-political life of the Muslims in Kerala. The Seventh and final chapter **Finding the Shore** is the major findings and conclusion of my Research.

Chapter - 2

Finding the Compass

Digging into every facet of migration related social change takes a great deal of effort. It requires, first of all, defining what 'migration' is, and secondly, how social life gets shaped by it. The concept of social change is discussed in detail and its scope is also defined. For a better read, this chapter is divided in to four progressive segments. At the outset, the concept of migration and various theoretical foundations figure for discussion. In this segment, a broad overview of migration and review of various types of migration theories is given in detail, and also emphasis is on the need for a multi disciplinary and interdisciplinary approach to the study, and theorization of migration. In the second segment, the phenomena of social change and its theoretical background is discussed in detail. In the third segment, the major factors that link migration to social change are explored. At the concluding part of this chapter, the theoretical framework of the present study is discussed. It also produces proof as to how the broad concepts of migration and social change go hand in hand apart from pointing out some theoretical complexities of theorizing migration and social change.

Migration

Migration is as old as man's history on this wonderful world to wander. Throughout the transition of human life, the phenomenon went on. Migration as part of human experience from the remote past to the present and on into the future (McNeill and Adams: 1978). Though human mobility was the characteristics of even the Stone Age men, the rapidness of industrialization and urbanization in the modern age has given it a big push. Today, modern means of fast and reliable transportation and cutting-edge communication help thousands of people leave their usual habitat to put better food on the table, explore new opportunities, in some cases to seek refuge and escape from the ill-treatment of the host countries. The present patterns of migration are fundamentally different from those in pre-industrial societies both in geographical scope and in intensity.

Through different growth phase of the development of history, man has been backpacking and making his way to explore what's written in his stars. The roving character, it is said, is inherent human nature not only in the need to search for food, pasture and resources but also the desire to cover and conquer. Population movements have been the carriers of innovation from one region to another. Migration and mobility at large have always been a part and parcel of stories heard about human beings but the nature and scope of migration have fundamentally changed over the past two centuries. The technological advancement which accompanied the rise of modern industrialist capitalism has been a key factor in facilitating large-scale migration, particularly through dramatic improvements in infrastructure and faster, safer and cheaper means of transport.

Meaning of Migration

Oxford dictionary defines 'migration' as the "movement of people to a new area or country in order to find work or better living conditions". Social, economic or political circumstance changes everywhere around the world and so does the need to move out. Thus, it results in permanent or temporary shift of people from one habitat to another. It can be within the borders of a country (internal migration) or between countries (international migration). Again, such a movement can take place in two different ways. Forced migration is the first case caused by factors like political pressures, religious prosecutions, natural calamities etc., and seeking refuge outside the place of origin. The second case of migration is voluntary in nature being caused mostly by economic considerations like material gains employment opportunities etc. Theodore Caplow (Caplow 1975:11) states that

"Migration is strictly speaking a change of residence and need not necessary involve any change of occupation, but it is closely associated with occupational shift from kind to another".

In most general sense, the word 'migration' is defined as the relatively permanent movement of the persons over a significant distance (Sillis 286: 41). A person goes to another country and put up there for the rest of his life is a migrant and one who pays a two-month visit to the nearest country is not. Between these two extremes lies a puzzling area of intermediate instances. But when we speak of migrant labor the connotation is not a permanent move from one area to another, but rather a permanently migratory way of life (Sillis: 286). According to National Sample Survey 2008, a migrant is defined as "A household member whose last usual place of residence, anytime in the past was different from the present place enumeration was considered as a migrant member in a household". Migration is the results of the behavior of individuals, but likewise it has a collective social form (Skeldon 1997:18). Migration thus can be analyzed at the individual or family level or at the level of the broader social group depending on what emphasis one gives to the key determining factors. Migrants are agents whose actions do have consequences, either intended or unintended upon social structure.

Theories of Migration

Migration on paper is essential in the sense that they help those who study human mobility within wider political, social, economic and cultural contexts. There is no painless process to theorize 'migration'. However, current patterns and trends in migration suggests that a full understanding of contemporary migratory process will not be achieved by relying on the tools of one discipline alone, or by focusing on a single level of analysis. It is a multifaceted phenomenon. Migration has its impact on every facet of human life. Theory comes handy here. Migration embraces all dimensions of social existence; and therefore demands an interdisciplinary approach. Efforts have been made to achieve this through interdisciplinary research teams, as well as through theoretical work designed with 'talk across disciplines' (Brettell and Hollifield: 2007). At present, there is no single theory widely accepted by social scientists to account for the emergence and extension of international migration throughout the world, only a fragmented set of theories that have developed mostly in isolation from one another, sometimes but not always segmented by disciplinary boundaries (Massey et al 1998: 17).

Multiple disciplines offer different theories of the causes and patterns of international migration. There is no single and coherent theory of international migration. The study of migration is productive only when we put together different branches of knowledge. There are a number of economic theories on migration. The central assumption of economic paradigm is that international migration is a mechanism to redistribute labor. Consequently, economic theories seek to explain labor migration that is the international movement of economically active individuals. Political paradigms of migration have also made several contributions to it. It attempted to explain not only why or not immigration occurs but, from a variety of perspectives the affect of international migration on the state and the influence of states on migration flows and the power structure and power relations of the state. Since the 1980s political scientists have been increasingly taking up the issue of migration as nation states as the primary unit of their analysis. (Messina and Lehav 2006:33). Sociological paradigms discuss the factors like the role of family, interpersonal connection of migrants, psychological factors behind the process of migration, the impact on the social structure and social paradigms etc.

Scholars of migration have tried to formulate theories based on different aspects on migration. As regards the origin of migration some works concentrates the decision making of the individuals and others concentrated on society–micro analytical and macro analytical respectively. Some other works used the term 'humanist' and 'determinist' to denote the same. In humanist approach the individual is the decision maker in the choice whether to migrate or not. In contrast, for the determinist, it is the society which he lives becomes the deciding factor. In short, the theories conceptualize the process of migration in four different levels of analysis i.e., the individual, the house hold, the national and the international. But in fact all these theories are interconnected. For example, while the individual acts to maximize income, naturally the families minimize risk, and that the context within which both decisions are made is shaped by structural forces operating at the national and international spheres.

Though the migratory movements acquired new dimensions since 18th century, very few theoretical formulations have been evolved for a long period (Joseph 2000: 11). Ravenstein, a German-born former cartographer for the British war office is remembered as the pioneer for the migration study, who provided a theoretical framework for migration[1]. Following Ravenstein a lot of literature has so far appeared concerning the spatial mobility of people. A number of theories were also put forwarded. Ravenstien's Law has been discussed, standardized and expanded by a number of researchers.

Several theoretical perspectives on migration came to top and there was a marked attention on the topic during twentieth century. However, they evolved in isolation from one another, and showed important differences in their level of analysis as well as paradigmatic and thematic orientation. One of the possible reasons for this lack of coherence is that migration has never been the exclusive domain of one of the social sciences, but has been studied by most of them. (Haas 2008: 11). To sum up, varieties of theoretical models has been proposed to explain why human migration begins and also each finally seeks to explain the same thing. Instead of going in to details of all migration theories, only the major theories on migration are discussed in this chapter.

Neoclassical Version

It is perhaps the oldest and well-known theory of international migration was developed originally to explain labor migration in the process of economic development. EG Ravenstein was the pioneer of the theory. He made the first scholarly contribution to migration which consists of two articles by the nineteenth century (Ravenstein1885: 167-227, Ravenstein EG. 1889: 214-301), in which he formulated his 'laws of migration' and his conclusion of the major cause of migration was economic reasons.

According to Ravenstein, migration between two places is always related to distance. Migrants move mainly over short distances; those going longer distances head for the great centers of industry and commerce. The movements to the trade hubs stepped up over time when transportation facilities grew greater in size. He pointed out that migrants move from areas of low opportunity to right set of circumstances with better pay packets. One of the factors affecting the choice of destination is distance. He also pointed out that the economic purposes are the major catalyst for migration. The main temptation for the movement of the people from rural to urban areas is mainly high wages and better opportunities (Ray 2003: 36). Since then, many scholars have introduced different formulations to uncover various aspects of migration.

Neoclassical Economics Theory

A number of early theories on migration surround around neoclassical economics. This theory is backed by the principle that migration occurs as a result of rational economic calculation workers do about the wage differentials, which results in the spatial movement of workers from low pay places to better pay places. This perspective, in which people are expected to move from low income to high income areas, has remained dominant in migration studies since Ravenstein (1885, 1889) formulated his laws of migration. The idea that migration is a function of spatial disequilibria constitutes the basic assumption of so-called 'push-pull' models which still dominate much gravity-based migration modeling as well as reasonable and non-specialist academic thinking about migration. Migration was thus labor reallocation in response to market demand. The neoclassical model works at both the macro and the micro level.

At the macro-level, neo-classical economic theory explains migration by geographical differences in the supply and demand for labor. The resulting differentials in wages cause workers move from low-wage, labor-surplus regions to high-wage, labor scarce regions. In some countries and regions, labor is abundant and capital is limited and consequently the wage level is low. In other countries the situation may be different: abundant capital, labor shortages and high wages. The result is that workers move from low-wage to high wage destinations. In doing so, however, they alter the dynamics of supply and demand for labor in both places, leading ultimately to the eradication of wage differentials, and therefore of migration too.

According to this theory, international migration is caused by geographic differences in the supply of and demand for labor. Neoclassical economists also believed that labor markets are the primary mechanisms by which international flow of labor are induced; other kinds of markets do not have much effect on international migration. (Massey and Joaquin 2006:37) It also explains that the elimination of wage differentials will end the movement of the labor, and migration will not happening in the absence of such differentials.

Corresponding to the macroeconomic model, in micro model migration is the result of decisions made by individual 'rational actors' who weigh up the pros and cons of moving relative to staying, based on plenty of information about the options. It is a model of individual choice. At the micro-level, neo-classical migration theory views migrants as individual, rational actors, who decide to move on the basis of a cost-benefit calculation. Assuming free choice and full access to information, they are expected to go where they can be the most productive, that is, are able to earn the highest wages. This capacity clearly depends on the specific skills of a person and the specific structure of labor markets. In this theory, international migration is conceptualized as a form of investment in human capital (Massey and Joaquin 2006:37). People choose to move to where they can be most productive, given their skills but before they can capture the higher wages associated with greater labor productivity they must undertake certain investments. According to this theory, international migration does not occur in the absence of differences in earnings and or employment rates between countries.

2.1. 8. The New Economic Theory of Migration

The new Economic Theory of Migration is at odds with the assumption and the conclusion of neo classical theory. The basic argument of this approach is that migration decisions are not made by isolated individual actors, but by larger units of related people like family and households. Unlike individuals, households are in a position to cut and control risks to their economic wellbeing by diversifying the allocation of household resources such as family labor. While some family members can be deputed for economic activities in the local economy, others may be sent to work in foreign labor markets. According to this theory, wage differentials are not an essential condition for international migration to occur; household may have strong incentives to diversify risks through transnational movement even in the absence of wage differentials.

There are two major aspects of the New Economics of Labor Migration. The first is to recognize that migration decisions: Who is going to migrate? Where is he going to? How long will he stay abroad? What will he do? etc., are not individual decisions but joint decisions taken within the family circle. Sometimes the scale of the decision-making unit moves further into the meso-scale of extended families and wider communal groups (Massey et al. 1998: 21). The second is that rational-choice decision-making is not only about wage and income maximization but also about income diversification and risk aversion[2]. New economic labor migration theories still largely fail to take into account many noneconomic factors that shape migration. Collinson (2009) proposes the need for a political economy approach to migration that links the analysis of local-level factors that influence people's migration decisions and livelihood strategies, with political, economic and social factors at various levels that affect the agency of the migrant.

2.1. 9. Dual Labor Market Theory

Being a micro level decision model, the new economic theory and neo-classical theories of migration focus on limited territories. Evidently, these theories shows to be true that individuals and the families are the crucial factors in these theories. There is headhunting in the wake of global economies opened due to industrial breakaway. Dual labor market theory argues that international migration stems from the essential labor demands of modern industrial societies. Michael J Piore argued that international migration is caused by a permanent demand for emigrant labor that is intrinsic to the economic structure of developed nations (Piore 1979). According to him, migration is not caused by push factors in the sending countries, but by pull factors in the host countries. This is linked to the presence of a dual labor market in advanced industrialized countries: a primary labor market of secure, well-paid jobs for native workers; and a secondary labor market of low-skill, low-wage, lacking security and normally foul shop floors or service sector, filled generally by migrant workers because such jobs are shunned by local workers.

2.1. 10. World System Theory

World systems theory appeared in the wake of dependency theory and built up a more complete and sophisticated historical analysis of the development and expansion of the global capitalist system from the sixteenth century on (Wallerstein 1974, 1979). As stated by world system theorists, the beginning of international migration is not due to the bifurcation of the labor market within particular national economies, but due to the structure of the world market that has been developing and expanding since the 16th century (Castells 1989 and Petras 1981). International migration is a natural outgrowth of distractions and displacements that inevitably occur in the process of capital development. It considers international migration as a natural outcome of capitalist market formation in the developing world; the incursion of the global economy into peripheral regions is the catalyst for international movement. As capitalism expanded outward from its core, a growing share of human population has been incorporated in to the world market economy. As land, raw materials and labor within peripheral regions come under the influence and control of markets, migration flows are inevitably generated, some of which always moved abroad (Massy1989:51, 670-685). Rather than adopting the narrow argument of theoretical exclusivity, it is better to adopt a broader position to understand the process of international migration.

2.1. 10. Dependency Theory

Dependency theory argues that migration is self-perpetuating, reproducing inequality through the mechanism of cumulative causation (Myrdal 1957; Petras 1981). Unlike the developmental framework where migration is positively linked to development (see de Haas 2001a for a review). This theory observes international migration as a part and parcel of the global geographic division of labor and of the historical process of subordinate incorporation of the underdeveloped world into the major capitalist economies (Morawska 2012: 60). This process dislocates millions of people in poor countries from their traditional way of life; they either migrate to urban areas within their own countries or are involved in international migration in search of the means of survival.

The historical-structural theories of migration (World System Theory, Dependency Theory and Dual Labor Market Theory) have common fundamental shortcomings. They regard migrants as 'little more than passive pawns in the play of great powers and world processes presided over by the logic of capital accumulation' (Arango 2004: 27). Three further drawbacks also can be observed when we look at the real world outcomes. First, migration flows are not all channeled along the pathways of capital penetration. Second, the agency of migrants is denied. Third, surprisingly little attention has been paid, by all the models reviewed thus far, to the role of the State in patterning migration flows.

2.1. 11. Network Theory

The focal point here is the collective agency of migrants and communities in organizing processes of migration and incorporation (Boyd 1989; 638-670, Portes and Bach 1985). Expatriates get connected with former migrants and non migrants in origin and destinations areas through ties of kinship, friendship and shared community origin. The networks form a catalyst of migration by cutting the risks and cost of movement and shooting up the expected net returns to migration. Network connection creates a form of social capital that people can draw upon to gain access to foreign employment. According to this theory, the cost and risk of migration will decline steadily and the possibility to get a better income or gain from such movements too.

Migrants' networks have been developing in three different levels. A person's individual migration-experience and worldliness promote migration of other people who are somehow connected to the expatriate. It should also rise with the quality of the social capital embodied in the relationship. Within households, we should also be able to identify the effect of social capital on individual migration behavior. In general, members of households in which someone has already migrated abroad should display higher possibilities of movement than from households without any migratory experience. Finally, at the community level, one should be able to observe the effect of the prevalence of network ties. People are more likely to migrate abroad if they come from a community where many people have migrated and where a large stock of foreign experience has accumulated than if they come from a place where international migration is relatively uncommon.

According to Boyd and Nowak (2012: 79-83), there are three main types of migrant networks: family and personal networks, labor networks, and illegal migrant networks. These scholars also highlight the gendered nature of all networks, and the often active role of women in developing and sustaining personal networks (2012: 83-86). Networks also make international migration much attractive and a strategy for risk minimization. When migrant networks are well developed, they put a destination job within easy reach of most community members and make emigration a reliable and secure source of income. Every new migrant expands the network and reduces the risk of migration. This phenomenon is very visible in Gulf migration from Kerala.

2.1. 5. Push-Pull Theory of Migration

The theory (Lee 1966: 47-57) states that migration comes to pass because of 'plus' and 'minus' factors in areas of origin and destination. People move world over driven by a set of push factors triggered from the country of origin, i.e., poverty, unemployment, landlessness, rapid population growth, political repression, low social status, poor marriage prospects etc., and pull factors operating from the place or country of destination i.e. better income and job prospects, comfortable and cushy jobs, better education and welfare systems, land to settle and farm, good environmental and living conditions, political freedom etc. In Lee's (1966) version of this model, there is also a set of 'intervening obstacles' which have to be overcome. They are; distance covered, cost of carrier, cultural roadblocks such as language and political obstacles such as international borders, immigration restrictions etc. Although Lee did not use the term himself, his analytical framework is normally referred to as the 'push-pull' model (Passaris 1989). Push-pull models identify different economic, environmental, and demographic factors which are expected to push migrants out of places of origin and attract them into destination areas (Hass, Hein De: 2010).

The conceptual framework of this theory is that push factors in countries of origin causes people to leave their country and pull factors attract migrants to certain receiving countries even though this model was developed with economic migration in mind and has its limitations. Although push factors are often responsible for migrants' decisions to leave their home country, it is the variation of pull factors that is widely seen as determining the direction of migration flows, i.e. influencing a migrant's choice of destination country. A review of the theoretical literature on migration produces five principal categories of pull factors– economic, historic, political, geographical, and policy related factors(Theileman: 2006: 442).

For various reasons, the analytical value of the push-pull model is limited. First, it is a static model which does not specify how migration affects the primary conditions under which it took place. Second, it is a descriptive, post-hoc device to explain migration, in which various 'migration determinants' at different levels of aggregation are lumped together in a relative arbitrary manner, without specifying or measuring their relative weight. Third, push-pull models often commit a classical "ecological fallacy" by confounding macro-level migration determinants (e.g., population growth, environmental degradation, climate change or variability) with individual migration motives. This also reveals the assumptions that particular factors (root causes) directly cause migration, without taking into consideration their interactions with other factors affecting livelihood. (Haas: 2010).

Analysis of Migration Theories

To state in words of one syllable, the subject matter of migration is too diverse and multifaceted to join up on a single paper. This has led some claim that migration is only weakly theorized (e.g. Arango 2004). The early theorizations were rather inflexible and hard to fit to each other, but more recent efforts to blend deductive with inductive reasoning have led to a variety of middle-range theorizations which reflects the realities of migration today. It has been demonstrated that, despite the relatively long tradition of research on migration, there is no single theory that captures the full complexity of migration and nor will there ever be.

Two very broad trends can be noted in the recent writings about migration by some of the most influential scholars in the field such as Stephen Castles (2010), Thomas Faist (2010) and Alejandro Portes (2010). The first trend is an attempt to rewrite migration within the wider phenomena of social change and social transformation, so that migration is not studied and theorized in isolation. Indeed, not only migration is caused by broad dynamics of national and global social change; but also, it is a part and parcel of that change. Castles (2010: 1596) advocates that migration studies need to be embedded in broader social theory, drawing on the full range of social science disciplines. He asserts, that "migration embraces all dimensions of human experience, and therefore demands an interdisciplinary approach".

2 .2 Social change

Change is always everywhere. An ancient Greek philosopher Heraclitus mentioned the fact in an emphatic manner as he says that it is impossible for a man to step in to the same river twice. It is impossible because in between the first and the second attempt, both the river and the men have already changed. Change is ever-present in the world, because change is the Law of universe. Similarly society is not at all stagnant phenomenon, but it is dynamic entity. Social change has occurred in all societies and at all times. The phenomenon of social change is not simple but complex. It is difficult to understand this phenomenon in its totality.

The term 'social change' is used to point out the changes that take place in human interaction and interrelations. 'Social change' refers to the modification which happens in life-patterns of people. This term is also explained that the changes in social structure including the social institutions, the social behavior or the social relations of a society and above all the nature of the community of people. Society is a web of social relationship and hence social change clearly means a change in the system of social relationship. Social relationship is understood in terms of social process and social contacts and social organization. Thus the term social change is used to desirable variations in social interaction, social process and social organization. (Rao 2005)

Social change includes any kind of transformation in the demographic, structural, cultural or environmental characteristics of a social system (Johnson, 2007:302-303). The definitions of 'social change' are highly diverse because their purpose is a social phenomenon, a social process that tends to have diverse dimensions and aspects, unfolding at different levels of generality. Different scholars have defined the term social change in deferent ways. M.E Jones defines 'social change' as "Social change is a term used to describe variation in, or modification of any aspects of social process, social pattern social interaction or social organization". Moore, for instance, defined 'social change' as a significant alteration of social structures, i.e. of patterns of social action and interaction (Moore 1967:03). Maclver and Page have given somewhat a comprehensive definition to social change as it goes like "Social change refers to a process reactive to several types of changes; to change in the manmade condition of life; to change in the attitudes and believes of men and to the changes that go beyond the human power to the biological and physical nature of things". H.T Majumdar defines Social change as a new fashion or style either modifying or replacing the old in the life of a people-or in the operation of society.

Theories of Social Change

All modern sociologists unanimously express their arguments on the naturalness and inevitability of social change in each human society. However, at the same time they project and advocate various theories of social change. Each theory seeks to explain the nature, reasons and scope of social change in a particular way. Sociologists, social anthropologists and historians have put forwarded numerous general theories of social change.

The general theories may conveniently be grouped in to five main categories.

(1) Evolutionary Theories

(2) Cyclical Theories
(3) Conflict Theories
(4) Functional theories
(5) Modernization Theories and
(6) Theories of Multiple modernity.

1. Evolutionary Theories

Evolutionary theories are based on the assumption that societies steadily change from simple beginnings into complex forms. Early sociologists believe that human societies evolve in a single and linear way. The well-known advocates of the Evolutionary theory of social change are Auguste Comte, Emile Durkheim and Herbert Spencer. According to them social change is the process of progress towards something better. They view change as positive and beneficial. Comte saw human societies as progressing into using scientific methods. Likewise, Emile Durkheim, one of the founders of functionalism, advocates societies as moving from simple to complex social structures. Durkheim interprets social mechanisms and the evolution of society through the prism of the evolutionary principle, and social progress through social differentiation. Herbert Spencer compared society to a living organism with interrelated parts moving toward a common end. In short, Comte, Durkheim, and Spencer proposed linear evolutionary theories, which mean that all societies pass through the same sequence of stages of evolution to reach the same end.

2. Structural Functionalist Theory

The Structural-Functional theory of social change has been a very popular theory of present times. It is strongly advocated by several sociologists, particularly by Tallcott Parsons and Morton. According to its proponents, every social system has two parts; one structural and the other functional. A structure is an arrangement or a unit for the performance of functions. Function is the consequent of the actions of structures. All the structures are closely related to each other and all the functions are interrelated and interdependent. Change in one leads to changes in others. Each structure serves its own function and at same time helps others to function.

According to Parson, the society as a whole is conceptualized into a system which consists of four subsystems interactive to maintain social order viz., social, economic, political and cultural subsystems. Changes in each of the subsystem generate effects and consequences in all the others. In this way the whole social system functions and undergoes social change. For example, a change in the marriage system from arranged marriages into love marriages leads to changes in caste system, family system, joint family system, rate of divorce and even religion. Just like any change in the economic structure of a society will make many changes in their Social relations and its political sphere.

Functional theorists are concerned with the role of cultural elements in preserving social order as a whole. Functionalists see society as a system in equilibrium. If some external force disrupts the equilibrium of the society, there takes place a counter-force for maintaining the social equilibrium. Parson's equilibrium model says that any change occurring in any part of the society is countered by adjustments in other parts. If this does not take place, the social equilibrium poses serious threats and several strains develop. Like evolutionary theorists, he believes that societies evolve from simple to compound societies. Functionalists assume that social institutions cannot persist unless they contribute to overall social integration. As social units multiply and specialized occupations tend to grow, it becomes necessary to coordinate all aspects of society.

3. Conflict theories

Conflict theories are concentrated on the role of social tensions and disregarding the influence of the technological progress or external influences in the area of social Change. In the classical Marxist theory, typical of the conflict perspective, social change takes place exclusively through conflict, being fraught with ambiguities of an economic and social nature. Marx held that human society passes through various stages, each with its own well defined organizational system. Each succeeding stage comes into existence as a result of conflict with the one preceding it. Change from one stage to another is due to changes in the economic factors namely the methods of production and distribution of material means of life. A change in the material conditions of life brings changes in all social institutions, properly system, state, religion and family.

From the economic point of view, Marx considers the origin of social disturbances as the means of production and explores the contradiction between production forces and production relations. According to Karl Marx, conflicts arises due to conflicts between unequal social groups and classes, inequality being fuelled by economic contradictions, which, ultimately, evolve into social contradictions calling for a change. Marx upholds that social inequalities typical of capitalism would end only when the working class had established the proletarian class. According to Marx, the proletariat is the historical agent of change, while the middle classes are the principal agent of social order. To sum up, in Marx's theory, all parts and phases of social life are dependent upon the economic factors.

4. Modernization Theories

Modernization theories emerged in the 1950s, explaining the development of industrial societies in North America and Western Europe, especially due to the rise of industrial capitalism since the 18th century. It is a grand theory encompassing different disciplines as it seeks to explain how society progresses, what variables influence that progress, and how societies can react to that progress. Modernization theory focuses specifically on a kind of modernization thought that probably originated in Europe during the 17th century, which brought social mores and technological achievements into a new epoch. It is the process of social change begun by industrialization (Macionis: 2006).

Modernization is ever present in society and has been for many years. It can be seen in every sphere of human society. It has been present ever since the dawn of human's appearance in the Universe. Every generation evolved and "bettered" themselves to some degree. Modernization theory tries to recognize the social variables which contribute to social progress and development of societies, and seeks to explain the course of social evolution. This theory not only stresses the process of change but also the responses to that change. It also looks at internal dynamics while referring to social and cultural structures.

The basic assumption of modernization theory by the advocates of this approach is that modernization is a total social process associated with economic progress. Among various writers, there are differences of opinion with respect to the meaning of modernization. For Lerner, modernization is the social process in which development is the economic component (Lerner 1967:21). Some writers stress structural aspects while for others regard the concept of modernization has to do with a transformation of culture and personality in, so far as it is influenced by culture rather than some aspect of social organization or of human ecology (Stephenson 1968:265).

Samuel P Huntington defines modernization as a multifaceted process involving change in all areas of human thought and actions. He further points out that the basic aspects of modernization are urbanization, industrialization, secularization, education and media participation. The total social transformation and universal assumptions of modernization theory encourage the attempt to relate to each other with the various types of change, within and between levels, through organizing principles emerge from the core definition of the modern that is adopted and certain a priory theoretical assumptions. Modernization theory encompasses many changes developed in individual attitudes, in social behavior, in economics and in politics. All these changes are related to one another.

5. Theories of Multiple Modernity

The past years have seen the emergence of numerous academic alternatives attempting to resolve the criticisms of modernity and to expand its horizon in explaining the phenomenon of social change. Theory of Multiple Modernity is one of the most influential among these. The concept of multiple modernity has emerged to challenge the dominant Euro-centrism and uni-linearity of traditional theories of modernity, and has led to renewed efforts to appreciate different routes of contemporary political and social developments. This theory argues that modernity continues to have an indisputable global impact, but that this impact is so radically mediated by the historical and cultural backgrounds of every society it encounters that it makes more sense to speak of the concept in the plural (Fourie, Elsje2010: 2).

Theories of Multiple Modernity, is comparatively a recent origin in social science discourses. The term was coined by sociologist Schmuel Eisenstadt in the late 1990s, who in many ways was the architect of the theory. Eisenstadt argues that the classical view on modernity, as derived from the western experience is not applicable to all modernizing societies, and that it needs to be proved by a concept of multiplicity. This is the reason that modernizing societies bring in their own socio-cultural influences that drive modernization, and that the western experience may merely serve as a reference point in the respective developments. The modernization process needs to be understood as the negotiation of multiple societal stakeholders about what makes society modern rather than as a historical consequence.

Eisenstadt discovered contrary to general scientific assumption; modernity or progress is not in the homogenous sense, but develops in heterogeneous way. The most significant contribution from Eisenstadt Multiple Modernity is that he identified the globalization impact opens new potential to develop different process of modernity across the globe. He also identified the role of new agencies, institutions and social movement responding to the impact as a part of dynamics modernity project. Multiple Modernity indicates that even though different societies develop their own distinct and unique ways of modernity; its movements will converge and connected to the whole project of modernity. The idea of multiple modernity assumes that the best way to understand the contemporary world indeed to explain the history of modernity is to see it as a story of continual constitution and reconstitution of a multiplicity of cultural programs.

Does migration change society?

Migration is, of course, change and it can lead, in turn, to further transformations in sending and receiving societies. It can influence the social relations, social values, cultural approaches and even political behavior and sometimes even strengthening the fundamental constitutive elements of society. Portes admits that the changes migration sets in train in less-developed sending societies may be deeper, for example 'the culture of sending regions and even entire nations may be thoroughly trans nationalized. Portes emphasizes the significance of time in the analysis of migration and its consequences.

Some changes may visible in a short span of time and some other transformation may be consume much more time.

The fundamental role of migration and remittances in social and economic reproduction of sending communities has been widely acknowledged (Heinemeijer et al. 1977; Klooster 2005). Migration also tends to affect socio-ethnic structures and political cultural spheres in sending communities. The influence of migration in every society is not in a single pattern. It is much different in different societies. Migration and remittances can have deep consequences for social, class and ethnic hierarchies in sending communities if lower status groups manage to migrate internally or internationally, which may upset traditional social hierarchies (Ilahiane 2001; Taylor, Moran-Taylor, and Ruiz 2006). Migration provides income for families which may undercut traditions of community service (Mutersbaugh 2002) and accelerate processes of family nucleation and individualization (de Haas 2006a).

Levitt (1998) coined the term social remittances to describe local-level, migration driven forms of cultural diffusion. Social remittances are the ideas, behaviors, identities and social capital that flow from receiving countries to sending countries or communities. Levitt emphasized the role of these resources in immigrant entrepreneurship, community and family formation and political changes. Migration does not only influence the processes of human development through individual social and financial remittances. Migration also affects social and political life in countries of origin in a broader sense. Migrants often play an important role in the civil society activities of countries of origin too.

Migration is also a potential force for structural change, because it can play an important part in altering the social and economic conditions in both in sending and receiving localities, regions and countries. In fact the impact of migration on the sending society is heterogeneous. It will affect in different ways in different countries or societies. The force of the impacts which brought by the migration will be different in different circumstances. It is highly depends on the character of the migration and the participation of the migrants.

Migration has the potential to affect the well-being of the migrants and the families, communities and nations they belong to. Migration-fuelled progress in living standards and well-being through better housing, sanitation, food and clothing etc:. Knowingly or unknowingly these changes leads to a much better social life of the concerned family or society. The remittances can also improve the economic status of households and communities. Migration also help to increasing people's capabilities to improve their livelihoods and in contributing to general economic growth and social change, the benefits of which may also grow to people in non-migrant households too.

However, it is important not to jump to the conclusion that migration has a direct positive impact on the overall well-being of people and their capabilities. The impact of migration on development of the society is mediated by other contextual factors too. Migration may have widely diverging-positive or negative-concrete impacts on the lives of people, depending on the type and causes of migration, the selectivity of migration, and, above all, the broader developmental context in which migration occurs.

Migration is an evolving social process that connects people, societies and cultures. The dynamism of human mobility creates new space for interaction among people of origin and destination countries.

The pivotal role of migration and remittances in social and economic reproduction of sending communities has been widely acknowledged (Heinemeijer et al. 1977; Klooster 2005). Migration also affects socio-ethnic structures and culture in sending societies in many ways.

Theoretical frame work of the study

We have examined various theories of Migration and social change. We have realized the fact that both concepts i.e., 'Migration' and 'Social Change' cannot be studied within the narrow framework of any single theory. Every theory has its own merits and demerits. Migration is a multidisciplinary and multifaceted subject and it cannot be put in the limited circle of a single theory. It is much complex in Kerala's Migration context. Among the above discussed theories of migration, we think The Network Theory and Push-Pull theory of

Migration is much more apt to explain the phenomenon of Gulf Migration from Kerala. Because the push factors in the state especially the unemployment and starvation were the two major factors, which forced many Keralites to cross the Arabian Sea and to the Arab coast. Enormous job opportunities and the better remuneration following the petrodollar prosperity and were the major Pull factors in Arab countries. At the initial stage the Gulf Migration was a safety valve for a huge number of Keralites to escape from the unending miseries in the state. Gradually The Migration gained momentum through the Network of the migrants.

Ethnic Network as a facilitator

The role of social networks is considered very important in both internal and international migration. The social networks help to probable migrants to find out new jobs in their destinations and ensure the all logistical support for the newly arrived migrants at the initial stages. The presence of persons from their place of origin (relatives, neighbors or friends) who are settled in the destination countries makes them comfortable. The ethnic networks that were built up facilitated the continuing migration of Keralites into Persian-Gulf countries.

The Mappilas have a special relationship with the Arab world because of the common heritage and Islamic identity. The religion has played as a catalyst in Gulf migration from Kerala Muslims. Ethnic networks were very vital in the Middle East since they created community enclaves within the destination which helped the unemployed youths from their own villages and made it possible for newcomers to take the risk of migrating to the Gulf even without having pre-arranged jobs. Most of the migration from these three villages took place as a result of friends, relatives or neighbors using their contacts with Arabs to arrange visas for new migrants.

This mode of recruitment has been taking kin, friends and other community members to gulf destinations instead of buying the services of any organized recruiting agencies who channelize information, provide resources, arrange legal papers like visa, emigration clearance etc. This network resolve distance related difficulties as well as those relating to legal and policy matters. Friends, kin or other community members of the sending community who have already migrated help the intending emigrants i.e. a former migrant becomes a recruiter. The specific ways in which such networks operate influence the shape and magnitude of the migration flow. It is in this way the gulf migration from Kerala has flourished till date.

At the initial stage, the Network was created in the limited circle of family. Then the chain of the network expanded in to local level and community level. The Network, which formed by the early migrants facilitated the migration process in a speedy way. This network operates in two different ways. When a migrant worker returns home, he brings with him Visa or NOC for the intending emigrants. This could either be for sale or as 'compliment' to his near and dear ones. Under the present state of labor-surplus situations, such compliments are considered as a gesture of obligation. These types of recruitment system have existed in many parts of Kerala. Although since the turn of the 1980s, institutionalized recruiting agents (legal or illegal) have started to function; the operation of this personal/ informal network has continued unabated. The personal/informal networks have foundations not only in the sending societies but have roots in the Middle East as well. The crucial aspect of migration is the obtaining of legal entry papers from the Middle East. With their excellent personal rapport and liaison with their employers, those migrants who are already employed in the Middle East are able to get the required papers in an easier manner.

Similarly the phenomenon of Migration, the migration caused Social Changes in Kerala is also very difficult to theorize .When it comes to the socio-political life of the Muslims in the state it will be much complex. Among the traditional theories of social change, the modernization theory is comparatively better to explain the social change in the state. Modernization theory is encompassing many changes including the individual attitudes, social behavior and the transformation in economics and political spheres. These all changes related to one another. But the problem is the modernization theory is not much powerful to explain the socio-political life of the Muslims in Kerala because of the euro centralism and the uni linear character of the analysis of the theory. According to the modernization theorists the idea of social change outside of the West is occurring as a consequence solely of the impact of the West and the modernity, in replacing tradition, would have the same effects across the globe. This Euro centric view of modernity has been questioned by many scholars due to its inability to explain the social development of various non Western societies in the World. So the migration related social change in Kerala is not systematically explained with this theory. Here the theory of Multiple modernities is the correct theoretical framework to analyze the socio-political life of the Muslims in Kerala. Advocates of multiple modernities argue that the traditional societies were not seen as stagnant, but as developing and transforming their own institutional and cultural contexts prior to the advent of Western modernity. Theory of multiple modernities also do not assume that the European experience is the most important and succinct manifestation and paradigm of the modernization process. That is why I think the Theory of multiple modernities is relatively more appropriate to explain the social and political life of the Muslims in Kerala. So I would like to seek support Eisenstadt's theory of Multiple Modernities as the base of the social Change in this study.

Notes

1. His hypothesis was first published in 1876 on Geographical Magazine. He also published another paper in the Journal of Statistical society in 1886. In this paper he pointed out that the economic causes is the important reason behind the decision to migrate.
2. Risk reduction is particularly appropriate in poor sending countries where 'market failures' (for instance, crop failure due to drought or hurricane, or sudden unemployment) cannot be compensated by savings, insurance or credit (because none of these are available).

Chapter - 3

Mapping the Footprints

With an irresistible instinct to spread wings, man has been crossing the borders of soil, sea and the sky since time immemorial promoting birth of civilizations on the river banks, on the top of hills and wherever he found water and food for survival. The chronicle of migrating Indians tells the same story though the pattern and implications are varying from time to time. As a huge reservoir of human resources, India has been a major source of skilled and unskilled labor resources for many countries all time. Though migration of Indians had been there very long before the colonial invasion to Indian subcontinent, it flourished with the British rule. The interminable needs of imperialists for workforce led to substantial recruitment of labor from India to plantations or mines in different British colonies: to far-away places such as Guyana, Jamaica, Trinidad and Fiji: to not so distant lands such as Mauritius, Malaysia, Singapore and South Africa; and even to neighboring countries like Ceylon (now Sri Lanka) and Burma (now Myanmar) (Davis, 1951: 87).

Indians trading across the Indian Ocean and over the Asian land masses is as old as ancient history. The trade relationship set the stage for movements beyond India by admittedly small numbers of Indians well before the period of European colonial intervention. However, they were very small in number. There were no streams of large scale in those days. It had two notable reasons. In the first place, during the pre-colonial period, Indians showed no notable tendency of expansion, power and colonization overseas. In the second place, it was the beliefs of the major religious community in India. As far as the Hindus are concerned crossing 'black waters' (kala pani) was traditionally regarded as full of danger (Jayawardena 1968: 428).

Slavery was put to an end in 1833, and laborers from different parts of India were recruited to various parts of the world like Fiji, Trinidad, Tobago, Burma, Malaysia, Mauritius, Guyana, Sri Lanka, West Indies and South Africa as plantation workers. Large scale migration from India had begun within the colonial era and continued after independence. It is possible to distinguish two waves of international labor migration from India during each of these periods.

The first stage was the indentured labor migration to plantations in several parts of British Empire. This process of migration came to an end with the outbreak of the First World War. The second wave of migration is known as the Kangani system of migration to Malaya and Ceylon. The third wave of mass migration from India started during the post colonial period. It was a skilled people's migration to the economically well developed nations. They were a new category; well educated people hailing from relatively well to do families. This groups of skilled migrants sought employment in foreign countries most in UK and US in administrative professional and technical positions. They included teachers, nurses and Engineers etc: (Nair 1986: 13). It was comparatively very small in numbers. The fourth and large stream of migration from India relates to the Arab World.

Migration during Colonial Period

Migration during colonial period took the form of brain drain; movement of administrators, military personnel and traders, migration based on inequality and coercion: slaves, indentured workers etc. (Cohen 1995). The mass human flow from India during this period is linked to the capital interests of the colonial rulers. This human flow was guided and controlled by the representatives of the colonial government. There were regular labor migrations from India to plantations and mines in the British colonies in the nineteenth century and early twentieth century. Those migrants were the pioneers of Indian labor migrants in countries like Malaysia, Guyana, Jamaica and Fiji, Singapore Sri Lanka and Burma.

Indentured Labor[1] Migration

The beginning of the 19th century was the setter of the trend for a dominant pattern of migration called Indentured labor migration. A new kind of recruitment developed in the wake of the colonial administration to employ laborers from the Indian subcontinent to the plantation fields in different parts of the colonial empire. Indentured labors were workers who had signed a contract to work in foreign countries for a specific period. This system was emerged following the abolition of slavery but the working atmosphere and the terms and condition for their job were not much better than a slave. It is common knowledge that the early migrants who had formed the basis of this so–called In-dian Diaspora formation mainly involved cheap manual workers leaving India in large numbers to meet the enormous quantitative demand for labor force for the plantations and mines in the colonies, im-mediately after the British abolished slavery in 1834– in the Caribbean (Guyana, Jamaica, Trinidad), the Pacific (Fiji), the Indian Ocean (Mauritius, South Africa, and East Africa), and south–east Asia (Malaysia, Singapore), as well as neighboring South Asian countries (Sri Lanka and Burma) – leading to what is sometimes also called the brawn drain.

The payment and employment conditions of the indentured labors were very disastrous. Wages were not sufficient and the general living standard was very pathetic, but the system was common in many parts of colonial world. A person became an indentured servant by borrowing money and then voluntarily agreeing to work until the debt was written off during a specified term. The indenture was a kind of contract by which the emigrant agreed to work for a given employer for five years, performing the tasks assigned to him for a specified wage. There after he might enter in to an ordinary contract of labor, or not work at all, and might change his residence. At the end of ten years he was entitled to a subsidized return passage.

The demand for Indian indentured laborers increased dramatically after the abolition of slavery in 1834. They were sent, sometimes in large numbers, to plantation colonies producing high value crops such as sugar in Africa and the Caribbean. In those days Thousands of Indian laborers had been imported to British plantation of various parts of the world. Many Indians were willing to work in those areas because of their extreme poverty and famine. Some of them migrated along with their family and some traveled alone. The indentured system of migration had been prevailing for almost eighty years, between 1834 and until the abolition on 1917. Davis (Davis 1951) estimates that about 30.2 million Indians had emigrated between 1834 and 1937. This scale of movement was as large as the European migration to the Americas in the 19th century(Sasikumar, Hussain: 2008).

Kangani System of Migration

Kangani recruitment system was primarily a personal or informal recruitment system and it became the preferred recruitment after 1910. This was more or less a south Indian phenomenon. The word 'Kangani' means "overseer or "foreman" in Tamil. A Kangani was usually a laborer who had already been employed in the plantation, and a man with some capital who lent his followers the expense of traveling to, and settle down on a plantation, who was also sent by his employer to recruit workers from his home village in India. He was paid commission on each laborer recruited. It was Kangani who negotiated with the manager about wages and work conditions on behalf of his men and could remove his followers to another plantation if the terms were not satisfactory.

The contract was also more often verbal rather than written, and the worker had the right to abandon his contract at a month's notice. This system was preferred because of the lower cost involved in sending a Kangani to recruit labor compared with the cost of indentured labor obtained through recruiting agencies. Kangani system also appealed to the planters because the prospect of workers absconding was less likely compared with the indentured system, since Kangani usually had a vested interest in ensuring that they did not. In early 1930s, under the impact of great depression, Kangani recruitment was suspended and it was formally abolished in 1938 (Gin, Ooi, Keat 2004:639).

Migration to East Africa

Migration to East Africa presents a third pattern: free migration of traders and skilled artisans who did not settle on the land as farmers or laborers. Indentured laborers were brought to East Africa to build the Mombasa railroad but few of them remained. Most of the present Indian population of Kenya and Uganda arrived after the railroad stimulated opportunities for trade. The emigration was not entirely unorganized. Those who established themselves brought down their fellow villagers, kinsmen, and caste-men. The new arrivals worked initially for their sponsors, but over a period of time branched out on their own, often financed by members of the local caste community. There is a basic similarity between free emigration and Kangani system that the emigrants were not unrelated individuals, as in the indenture system, but constituted self-regulating groups recruited on the basis of kinship, caste, and village of origin.

Table -3(1)

Year	*USA*		*UK*		*Canada*	
	Indian immigrants	*% of Indian immigrants*	*Indian immigrants*	*% of Indian immigrants*	*Indian immigrants*	*% of Indian immigrants*
1995	34748	4.8	4680	8.4	18262	8.6
1996	44838	4.9	4620	7.5	21291	9.4
1997	38048	4.8	4645	7.9	19615	9.1
1998	36414	5.6	5430	7.8	15376	8.8
1999	30157	4.7	6295	6.5	17458	9.2
2000	41903	5.0	8043	6.4	26126	11.5
2001	70032	6.6	7280	6.8	27904	11.1
2002	70823	6.7	8005	6.8	28838	12.6
2003	50228	7.1	11460	8.0	24593	11.1
2004	70151	7.3	11870	8.0	25576	10.9
2005	84681	7.5	-	-	33146	12.6

Sources: USA: Yearbook of Immigration Statistics, Office of Immigration Statistics, U.S.

Department of Homeland Security; UK: Home office, Government of United Kingdom; Canada. Citizenship and Immigration Canada. OP sited Sasikumar and Zakir Hussain (2008), Managing International Migration from India: Policies and Perspectives, ILO Asia Pacific Working Paper Series.

Migration after Independence

The pattern and dimension of international labour migration from independent India has been characterized by significant transformations over the past half a century (Nayyar, 1994; Indian

Council of World Affairs, 2001; Sasikumar, 2001; Srivastava and Sasikumar, 2003). Since independence, two distinct types of labor migration have been taking place in India. The first is characterized by a movement of persons with technical skills and professional expertise to the industrialized countries like the United States, Britain and Canada which began to proliferate in the early 1950s. It was comparatively much less in number. The second type of migration pertains to the flow of labor to the oil exporting countries of the Middle East which acquired substantial dimensions after the dramatic oil price increases of 1973. The nature of this unprecedented wave of migration is strikingly different, as an overwhelming proportion of these migrants are in the category of unskilled workers and semi-skilled workers skilled in manual or clerical occupations.

Skilled Migration to Western Countries

The exodus of talent and highly skilled professionals to the developed countries compri-sing doctors, engineers, scientists, teachers, architects, entrepreneurs, and so on appeared in Independent India in the second half of the twentieth century (Khadria, 1999, 62– 64). But it was gained momentum in the first half of the 1990s when the Government of India decided to enter in to the Neoliberal world order. It is striking to note that there has been a further increase in the number of Indians immigrating on a permanent basis to the Western industrialized countries since turn of the 21st century. For instance, in the case of the USA, this proportion which had more or less hovered around 5 per cent during 1995-2000 registered rapid increases during 2000-2005 to reach 7.5 per cent by 2005. Similarly in Canada, the proportion of Indians as percentage of the total immigrants which averaged around 9.5 per cent during 1995-1999, rose up to an average of nearly 13 per cent during the 2000-2005. In the case of United Kingdom, the proportion of Indians which had indicated a declining trend from 1995-2002 (from around 8 per cent to 6.8 per cent) registered an increase reaching 8 per cent in 2004 (Table 3:1).

The skilled migration became more prominent with the mass migration of the IT workers, and nurses to the Western Europe and US as well as the oil rich Arabian countries. In the developed countries today, the focus on the Indian skilled migration remains in the United

States, with up to 80 per cent of Indian skilled migration to all developed countries (Binod 2006: 5). However, this type of migration to the developed countries was very much limited due to the highly selective nature of the immigration rules in the host countries and the limited supply of eligible skilled manpower ready to move out of India (Tinker, 1974: 163-193).

Migration to the Gulf Countries

The mass migration of Indians in modern times and their permanent settlement in different parts of the world is a surprising phenomenon. Migration to the Persian Gulf, which started at a massive rate during the 1970s, is the second wave of migration on a big scale from the post-independent India. The contact and contract with the Persian Gulf region in terms of movement of people had begun though in small numbers-long ago, but it developed spontaneously and its ethnic composition has markedly changed after the emergence of oil (UMI 1998: 35. Migrant labor flows into the Gulf region were considerably accelerated by the dramatic oil price increase in 1970s. The region's dependence on foreign workers dates to the oil induced economic boom which followed the initial discovery of oil on the Gulf shores in the early part of the twentieth century. The development of the oil industry during this period had provided an additional need for workers in the clerical as well as skilled and semi-skilled manual occupations. Demand for workers also increased due to the development of trade, prosperity in commerce, boom in business, and the emergence of different kinds of service sectors in the Gulf. This has facilitated the demand for all kinds of workers in the Gulf countries since 1973.

Indians were mainly recruited for the clerical and technical positions of the oil companies in the Persian Gulf countries after oil was discovered in the region in 1930s. Though they were very minimal in number, the situation has changed dramatically by the next decade. Between 1948 and the early 1970s, these numbers gradually increased from about 1,400 to 40,000 (Binod 2006: 11). The oil companies were obliged to recruit large number of foreign workers in the oil industries since the local human resource available in the region had minimal expertise in industrial employment. Most of those foreign labors were recruited from British India. Since the mid 1970s, there was a sudden rise in the flow of skilled, semi-skilled and unskilled workers to the Gulf countries due to the emergence of large scale construction works in the region. In the flow of labors, India has been enjoying a prominent position to become the largest single expatriate community in all the GCC countries. In 1975, just after the sudden hike in oil price, Indian expatriates constituted 39.1 percent while Pakistanis 58.1 per cent and other Asians 2.8 percent of the total non–Arab expatriate in the in six Gulf countries. Since then, Indian migration has overtaken that of Pakistan and other Asian countries of origin. Despite some rise and falls in the outflow of the Indian labours to the Arab world, the statistics indicates that the actual numbers have been increasing since 1970s. The number of Indians in the Gulf region was 4.2 thousand in the year 1976 which increased to 677 thousand in 2006. By the 2011, Indian population in the Gulf has risen up to 3.318 million which is now estimated to have crossed 3.5 million.

Table 3:2: Stocks of Indian Migrant Population in the Gulf Countries, Selected years: 1975–2001

Country	*1975*	*1983*	*1987*	*1991*	*2001*
Saudi Arabia	34,500	270,000	380,000	6,00000	1500,00
U A E	107,500	2,50000	2,25000	400,00	950,00
Oman	385000	1,00000	184,000	2,20000	3,12000
Kuwait	32105	115,000	1,00000	88,000	295,000
Qatar	27,800	40,000	50000	75,000	1,31000
Bahrain	17250	30,000	77,000	100000	1,30000
Total	257,655	805,000	1016000	1483000	3318000

Sources: Rahman (1999), and Rajan (2004).

In the initial decades of oil boom, nearly 94.3 per cent of the total clerical and technical employees of leading oil companies were Indian labours. In the case of another leading oil company in the region, Kuwait Oil Company, Indians accounted for 85.6 per cent of the total clerical, foreman and technical staff of company in 1949 ((Seccombe and Lawless:1986). Proximity of Indian subcontinent to Gulf and British ownership of the Oil companies were two major catalysts for the large-scale recruitment of workers from Indian sub-continent in Gulf. Geographical proximity made migration easier and India being under the colonial rule, the leading oil companies, which were primarily British, hardly faced any procedural deterrents in transporting workers on a formal basis. In addition to the formal recruitment channels, a large number of undocumented Indian workers reached the shores of Gulf through informal means of transport.

Table 3:3: Annual Labour Outflow from India Destination-wise from 2008-2012

Sl. No.	*Country*	*2008*	*2009*	*2010*	*2012*	*2012*
1.	Bahrain	31,924	17,541	15,101	14,323	20,150
2.	Kuwait	35,562	42,091	37,667	45,149	55,868
3.	Oman	89,659	74,963	1,05,807	73,819	84,384
4.	Qatar	82,937	46,292	45,752	41,710	63,096
5.	S. Arabia	2,28,406	2,81,110	2,75,172	2,89,297	3,57,503
6.	U. A. E.	3,49,827	1,30,302	1,30,910	1,38,861	1,41,138
	Total	818315	592299	610409	6,03159	722139

http://www.mea.gov.in/images/pdf/annual-report-2012-13.pdf,
Source: Emigration Services Division, MOIA

Gulf Migration from India Post 1973

Although labor migration from India to Gulf countries had started since 1930s, the process gained momentum with the oil price increase during 1973-74 and 1979. The oil price hike marked enormous growth in the demand for foreign labours in the oil exporting states of Arab Gulf. The scale of labor migration to Gulf was closely linked to the increase in oil revenues and the unprecedented rate of investment in the domestic industry and infrastructure of the oil states. These states were not able to meet the growing labour demand with their limited human resources. Accelerated economic growth and the subsequent growth in the construction sector generated an unprecedented demand for labour far beyond the capacity of the local labour market.

The sudden spurt in demand for human resources became a boom for labour surplus economies, both within the Arab region and outside it. The decade since 1973-74, saw a dramatic increase in the number of migrant workers in almost all the oil exporting Gulf States. The flow of Asian labours to the Gulf gained considerable momentum since 1973-74, and reached its peak during the period 1977-82, when the developmental activities in industry and infrastructure were at a maximum in the Gulf.

The lion share of Indian migrants in the Gulf has comprised of the semi-skilled and unskilled workers. Around twenty five percent of the migrants were only white collar workers and professionals until the last decades of twenty century. However, this proportion more or less resumed, although some changes might have taken place due to the demand tilting more towards skilled professionals, as infrastruc-ture development progressed in the Gulf in the initial decades of the 21th century. Majority of unskilled workers have been working in construction sector. The rest of them are workers like housemaids, cooks, bearers, gardeners, etc. has been large, though systematic all–India data are not easily available, except for the state of Kerala.

Unskilled and semiskilled workers work-ing in infrastructural and development projects generally live in fed-up condi-tions and are accommodated in small overcrowded rooms in the labor camps. Often toilet and kitchen facilities are inadequate, and working conditions are harsh. Thus, adverse working condition, unfriendly weather, inability to participate in social and cultural activities, and long periods of separation from families and relatives leading to emotional deprivation are known to have wrecked the lives of low skilled Indian workers in the Gulf (Zachariah 2002: 17).

State-Wise Distribution of Emigrants from India

Job opportunities in Gulf have not been reflected in all parts of India at the same way and at the same time. There were wide differences among the states in with regard to their contribution of migrants to Gulf countries. It was only a few states that accounted for bulk of the labour migrants from India. For example in the early phase of the emigration process in 1977, Kerala occupied a special status as it accounted for 63 per cent of the total emigrants from India to the Gulf (IMF Survey: 1978). But this monopoly has been challenged by the states like Tamlnadu and Andra Pradesh. The share of Kerala among Gulf migrants has gone down since more states began to utilize Gulf labour market.

Though the lion share of Indian migrants are from the three states; Kerala, Tamil Nadu, and Andhra Pradesh, most of them mainly originat-ed from Kerala. This had led to the establishment of a separate ministry for non–resident Keralites, and three international airport at Thiruvananthapuram, Kochi and Kozhikode within the area of mere 38,863 Square Kilometer. Some of the other states having sizeable number of total labour emigrants to Gulf are Karnataka, Maharashtra, Punjab and Rajasthan (Khadria 1978: 26). The emigration clearance data gives an underestimate of migrating Keralite workers to Gulf because a university graduate is exempt from emigration clearance, and the number of such graduates is very high among the Kerala migrants to the Gulf.[2]

Table: 3:4: Workers Granted Emigration Clearance of Government of India, by Major Indian States, 1990–2012

States	*1995*	*2000*	*2005*	*2010*	*2012*
Kerala	165,629	69630	125075	1,04,101	98,178
Tamilnadu	65,737	63,878	117050	84,510	78,185
A.Pradesh	30284	29,999	48498	72,220	92,803
Karnataka	33496	10927	75384	17,295	17,960
Maharashtra	26312	13,346	29289	18,123	19,259
Others	93876	55402	153557	345107	440656
Total	415334	243,182	548853	641356	747041

Source: Author. Various Annual Reports of the Ministry of Labour, Government of India, as cited in Rajan (2003, ESCAP) for data till 1999; GOI, MOIA, *Annual Reports* 2004–5, 2005–6, for 2000–05. http://www.mea.gov.in/images/pdf/annual-report-2012-13.pdf

Notes

1. Indentured labour, one form of contract labour, was common in North America in colonial times. A person became an indentured servant by borrowing money and then voluntarily agreeing to work off the debt during a specified term. In some societies indentured servants probably differed little from debt slaves (i.e., persons who initially were unable to pay off obligations and thus were forced to work them off at an amount per year specified by law).-britanica .com
2. Southern states such as Kerala, Tamil Nadu and West Bengal have highest number of graduates in the country. There are no data on the state level exemption of emigration clearances but at an all–India level, it has shown an increasing trend during the last 10 years.

Chapter - 4

Bridging the Gulf

There has been a long, strong and still going tradition of migration about Kerala. Post colonial period is marked with the traces of travel Keralites made to Europe, UK, Africa, US and Far East. But such migration was very limited in number and had little impact on the state and society. However, cruise to Gulf destinations has been bringing home Dinars, dates and delight as flights touching down with gulf expatriates on board. Gulf migration has had its impact on every facet of the social life of Kerala. Emigration to the Gulf from India is by and large is a Kerala phenomenon (Joseph 2000: 66). Though many Keralites saw shores of Gulf greener and moved there even prior to the oil boom period, the flow was in high gear during the period of 1970 to 1990. Still the Arabian blue sea and its skies are busy with moving men, women and children. There are a number of studies conducted by the Government agencies and researchers to estimate the number of emigrants from Kerala to Gulf countries which reveal that number of emigrants has been increasing persistently even if there has been a decline in the rate of growth.

The trade tradition and relation of Kerala with various Arab countries since ancient past dating back to the pre-Christian era, is yet another vital point to migration study. Merchants from Arab world used to frequent South Indian ports like Quilon, Calicut etc., and engage in trade with India. Rice, spice and saleable merchandise moved off its shore to dot Kerala as a favorite destination in the world trade map. Syrian Christians and Mappila Muslims of Kerala, also claim ethnic connection with West Asian countries on a limited scale (Joseph

2000: 67). The links of Gulf trade connections were maintained even after the establishment of the European hegemony in the Indian subcontinent. Hajj pilgrims from India used to congregate in the Arab land. There are Muslims in the state who travel to work Gulf and perform Hajj. They find it a great accomplishment in their life.

Migration to Gulf regions in the modern period had its beginning, though on a small scale, when oil companies were open in the 1930s. It was very minimal in the initial years of oil exploration in the Middle East and gained momentum by 1970s. Started off with an unprecedented increase in oil prices in the early 1970s, there has been a large outbound drain from India to the Middle East. Kerala has been a major labor exporter to the Middle East ever since the very early days of Gulf migration. Although the state's population comprised only 3.43 per cent of the population of the country in 1990 (Prakash, 1994: 43), 35 to 50 per cent of the migrants from India were from this state (Gulati and Modi, 1983:58; Nair, 1989:343; Prakash, 1998).

The number of migrants has been increasing steadily even if there is a decline in the rate of growth in emigration to the Gulf (Table 4.1). According to an unofficial estimate, there were around 1.86 Lakhs Keralites, in the Gulf region during the year 1980, which jumped to 2.30 Lakhs in 1981 (Nair: 1983). A statewide survey conducted in 1992-1993 found that 23 per cent of households reported having at least one member working outside the country at one time or another.

Table 4.1: Figures of Migration from Kerala to Gulf

Year	*Number of Migrants*	*Year*	*Number of Migrants*	*Year*	*Number of Migrants*
1982	230740	1992	631703	2002	1717695
1983	274804	1993	754544	2003	1838478
1984	273342	1994	819025	2004	1900113
1985	313980	1995	957388	2005	1990441
1986	329083	1996	1062376	2006	2093520
1987	364909	1997	1178589	2007	2165782
1988	405513	1998	1318489	2008	2193412
1989	449611	1999	1412649	2009	2247678
1990	510214	2000	1501917	2010	2321750
1991	566668	2001	1600465	2011	2330860

Source: Zachariah and Rajan (2010), p. 25 and (2012), p. 26.

Another survey conducted in 1998, estimated that there were thirty-three international migrants for every one hundred households (Zachariah, et al.,1999: 4). Ninety six percent of these international migrants were probably in the Middle East (Banerjee 1997: 3).

Kerala Migration Survey 2014 quoted a figure of 23.63 Lakhs outbound emigrants. The corresponding number was 13.62 Lakhs in 1998, 18.38 Lakhs in 2003, 21.93 Lakhs in 2008 and 22.81 Lakhs in 2011. This point to the fact why there has been more addition of careers to the fleet to take off with more passengers. Migration from Kerala has been increasing since 1998. The info graphic illustrates the phenomenal jump of figures from 1998 to 2014 (Fig. 4.1).

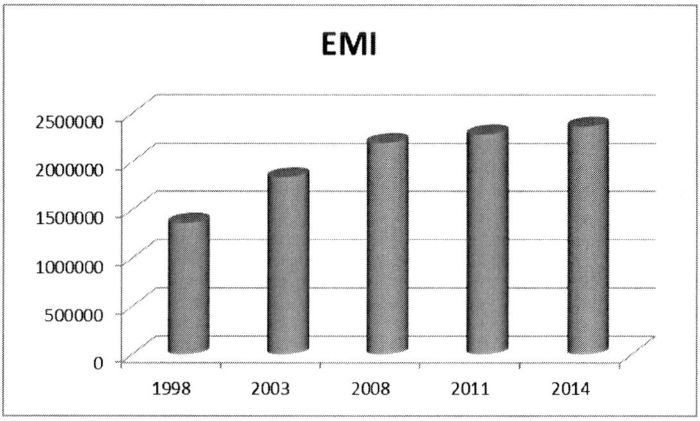

Source: Kerala Migration Survey 2014.

Figure 4.1: Number of Emigrants (1998-2014)

District-wise Distribution of Migrants

The northern districts of Kerala lead the trend in sending more job-seekers to Gulf. Close to 40 percent of emigrants from Kerala to Gulf region, hail from the three adjacent districts in the state i.e., Malappuram, Kozhikode and Kannur. In 2014, about 19 percent of the households had an emigrant in Kerala. 34.9 percent households have at least one migrant in Malappuram, among fourteen districts and the lowest proportion is in Idukki that is 6.9 percent (Table 4.1).

Table 4.2: Percentage of households with at least one migrant

Districts	*Household %*
Thiruvananthapuram	17.4
Kollam	20.0
Pathanamthitta	27.2
Alappuzha	14.1
Kottayam	12.4
Idukki	6.2
Ernakulam	12.7
Thrissur	19.2
Palakkad	9.9
Malappuram	34.9
Kozhikode	20.2
Wayanad	9.2
Kannur	28.9
Kasaragod	22.8
Kerala	19.0

**Source:* Kerala Migration Survey, CDS 2014.

As stated already, Malabar region has the big share (forty percent) of migrants. Malappuram stands out with 18.8 percent of the total migrants from the state followed by Kannur, The district is ahead of the curve Trivandrum and Kozhikode (Table 4.2). However, Idukki (0.30 percent) bucked the trend in the emigration process from Kerala. It might be due to the fact that the district is the major plantation area of the state and also accounts for the highest percentage of tribal population (Zachariah and Irudaya Rajan (2010).

Table 4.3: Distribution with district of origin

Districts	*No. Migrants*
Thiruvananthapuram	248852
Kollam	197014
Pathanamthitta	137730
Alappuzha	89905
Kottayam	110411
Idukki	23945
Ernakulam	186765
Thrissur	224978

(Contd...)

Palakkad	69186
Malappuram	444100
Kozhikode	224638
Wayanad	20511
Kannur	290335
Kasaragod	93598
Total Kerala	2361968

**Source:* Kerala Migration Survey, CDS 2014

Religious composition

Muslims are the major share of Gulf migration given the religion-wise distribution of the migrants from the state. Many studies bring the fact to fore that more Muslims go, work or do business to play a good-size in Gulf migration. Following Muslims, Latin Catholic Christians, Ezhavas and other communities sent sizable number of members to the Gulf region in the early phase of emigration. According to the study by Prakash (1978) 12, about 74.74 percent (71 out of 95 households) of the emigrants from Kerala were Muslim where as it was 78.0 per cent as per the study by Nair, (1986) even though the population share is only 26.5 (Population Census 2011) of the total population of Kerala.

Table 4.4: Muslim Population in Kerala 2001-2011

		2001			*2011*		
Sl. No.	*District*	*Total pulation*	*Muslim poulation*	*%*	*Total Population*	*Muslim Population*	*%*
1.	Trivandrum	3234707	420512	13.34	3307284	397170	12.1
2.	Kollam	2584118	473927	18.34	2629703	522804	19.9
3.	Pathamthita	1231577	56106	4.58	1195537	27124	2.3
4.	Alappuzha	2105349	207587	9.86	2121943	389023	18.3
5.	Kottayam	1952901	116588	5.97	1979384	57359	2.9
6.	Idukki	1128605	81147	7.19	1107453	86893	7.8
7.	Ernakulam	3098378	450504	14.54	3279860	454401	13.8
8.	Trissur	2975440	488865	16.43	3110327	547838	17.7
9.	Palakkad	2617072	703469	26.88	2810892	895857	31.8
10.	Malappuram	3629640	2487392	68.53	4141956	2971927	70.9
11.	Kozhikode	2878498	1078573	37.47	3089543	1093027	35.4
12.	Wynadu	786627	211367	26.87	816558	268880	32.9
13.	Kannur	2412365	666536	27.63	2525637	656824	26.0
14.	Kasargode	1203342	412867	34.31	1302600	547651	42.0
Total	Kerala	31838619	7641268	24.0	33387677	8856778	26.5

Source: Census of India 2001 and 2011.

A recent study has also submitted the proof of the dominance Muslim community holds in the Gulf migration as the proportion of Muslims was 43.6 percent while the percent of Hindus and Christians was 36.4 and 20.0 respectively (Zachariah and Rajan, 2012) 14. Around 37.2 per cent of Muslim households have one or more emigrants (2014), but the corresponding ratio is only 12.7% among Hindus and 19.5% among Christians. (Table: 4.3)

Table 4.5: Per cent of Households with an Emigrant (Religion-wise) 2014

	Hindus	*Christians*	*Muslims*	*Total*
Trivandrum	16.5	15.7	25.0	17.4
Kollam	18.0	24.4	27.1	20.0
Pathanamthitta	21.3	34.8	26.9	27.2
Alappuzha	11.9	19.8	100.0	14.1
Kottayam	8.7	19.3	8.6	12.4
Idukki	4.0	8.3	6.3	6.2
Ernakulam	10.5	14.3	18.0	12.7
Thrissur	15.9	19.1	30.8	19.2
Palakkad	5.5	8.8	23.9	9.9
Malappuram	12.8	44.4	41.3	34.9
Kozhikode	11.0	20.8	34.8	20.2
Wayanad	2.7	8.5	23.7	9.2
Kannur	17.8	25.0	57.8	28.9
Kasaragod	11.9	11.5	44.4	22.8
Kerala	12.7	19.5	37.2	19.0

District-wise religious composition of emigrants from Kerala shows that Muslims form majority of the emigrant population in the district like Malappuram (86 percent of the total emigrants) and Kozhikode (60 percent). The proportion of Christians is higher in the Ernakulum district (54 percent) while the share of Hindus is higher in the Thiruvananthapuram district (64 percent) (Zachariah and Rajan, 2012).

Dream Destinations

As far as Kerala migrants are concerned, the first choice has so far been Gulf countries. According to Kerala Migration Survey, conducted by Centre for Development Studies Trivandrum in 2014, around the

90% of the labor migrants from Kerala has been working in six Gulf countries (Table 4.8). United Arab Emirates, which attracted 38.7 percent of Kerala emigrants, is the first best choice with respect to emigration among all countries (Figure 3.4 and 4.3). Saudi Arabia comes in the second position with 25.2 percent of the emigrants from the state. Saudi Arabia was the prime destination of Kerala migrants in the early phase of emigration. But the Saudi's share had been down by late 1990s and UAE became the main destination of the Migrants from Kerala. The remaining strength of Kerala migrants has been shared by other four countries that are Kuwait, Bahrain, Oman and Qatar.

Table 4.6: Preferred Destinations of Gulf migrants from Kerala 2014

Countries	*Number*	*Percentage*
United Arab Emirates	886968	37.5
Saudi Arabia	514976	21.8
Oman	185996	7.9
Kuwait	180765	7.6
Bahrain	146472	6.2
Qatar	104623	4.4
Other West Asia	13368	0.6
Sub Total	2033168	86.0

*Kerala Migration Survey, CDS 2014.

Muslims in Kerala always moved and made themselves at home in faraway countries. They went to many parts of the world for a better living back home. Muslims rose culturally and economically through the process of migration. Migration has played a decisive role in the entire development of the Muslims in Kerala. This very fact is as clear as day and observable in the case of Gulf migration. Not only the economic prosperity and the socio-political development, but also Muslims are enlightened in the wake of Gulf migration. Muslims have an edge over the rest of the communities in migration to the Gulf region for a variety of reasons, historical, cultural and economic besides of course the religious factors (Nair 1986: 31).

The warm and welcoming relation between Malabar and Arab world is as old as the trade links both sides had during the centuries immediately preceding the advent of European trading companies in

16th century. Arab merchants came to Malabar and maritime trade between Kerala and Arab world bore fruit in the initial decades itself following their arrival. There existed a monopoly of Arab traders in Calicut and nearby areas. Arabs even found brides among native Muslims and there used to be a cultural merger through marriages. Such a wedding unions grew in number and it led to thinning the cultural barriers between Arab world and Kerala. Seemingly, the religious affinity has so far contributed a lot to this process. In the course of time when the reverse direction of migration happened, Muslims from Kerala began to migrate to the Arab countries in the following years. One cannot read the Gulf migration from Kerala in 1970s, without understanding the pattern of human migration from India to other parts of the world. The age-long trade relation with the outside world especially with the Arabs, prove to be a factor to picture how well Muslims from Malabar went around the world make home away from home. Many of the Muslims who lived in the coastal belts were in constant touch with them for several centuries through trading and matrimonial relations (Muhammed 2002: 48). This was another favorable factor for migration. The migratory nature inherent in the genes of coastal area population is acclaimed by a famous writer Sihabudheen (Sihabudheen 2008: 21). It is to bear in mind that neither all states in India nor all districts in Kerala had the trend during teething years of migration. Religions which are earlier experience of international migration and communities which had affinity of some type or other with the Arab world must have been the harbingers. Other communities, other regions and other countries must have joined the process later in the light of the experience of the pioneers (Nair 1986: 07)

Muslims in Kerala were in the vanguard of migration for a variety of historical and religious reasons (Mathew and Nair: 1978: 01). In fact, migration of Muslims from Kerala to Gulf regions had begun as far back as 1940s, but it became a large and steadily swelling flow only since early 1970s. One of the noteworthy characteristics is that minority communities like Muslims and Christians were the major proportion. Castes among Hindu community like Nairs and Bhrahmins were rare. This aspect of migration denotes two important points. First, emigration at the initial phase was a game risking life. It was both adventurous and the result was uncertain. The castes among Hindu, who did not have the tradition of taking a cruise or enterprising ventures, naturally, didn't think over it.

Muslim migrants, however, with regard to work experience and earning status were marginally better than others. This was quiet expected because Muslims in general, drop-outs from schools at a relatively low-age took to every sundry economic activities in fishing, trading and other petty businesses (Nair 1986: 19). Quoting Marx Weber, Dr. K.K.N Kurup shows this as the example for the influence that religion plays in the industrial development of a region (Kurup 1971 : 53). Secondly, migration was an escape and exit from the existing socio-economic conditions that existed in Malabar. The life experience of the Muslims in the region was lamentable compared to others. Muslims, at that critical point, were pressed to move seeking a pot of gold at the end of the rainbow.

As we noted earlier, in all the international migrations barring the professional migration, Muslims in Kerala especially from Malabar, were in the front where as migration to advanced countries in the west as we noted earlier, four-fifth of the migrants were from Travancore-Cochin region. A distinctive characteristic of migration to Gulf countries is a near absence of highly qualified manpower in the flow, in countries in the West (Radhakrishnan and Ibrahim 1981:19). When migration to advanced developed countries was a matter of highly educated in Kerala, emigration to Gulf was the concerns of the low-educated and illiterate. So in sharp contrast to the views expressed by the previous studies, one of the incentives of the migration from Malabar was not the progress in education but the relative backwardness.

The religious and ethnic connections have also played a dominant role in the migration to Arab world. "When faced with general economic pressure to migrate, individuals tend to choose countries that have close relationship with this (Psuda 1995: 08). Muslims in Kerala is an external symbol of the state's contact with West-Asian countries. There were Mappilas of Malabar, both the decedents of the Arab through local women and converts among local people (Sha 1975: 3) So it is quiet natural that the Muslims became the pioneers of migration to West Asia. Transnational socio-economic-political-historical linkages between sending and receiving countries are important determinants when understanding how migration flows are constituted (Psuda 1995: 08). The migration of Brazillian Nikkeirjin to the distant land of Japan is an example for this aspect of migration. Instead of moving the nearest advanced countries Brazilians, they opted to migrate Japan. This explains the impact or historical connection and linkages between Brazil and Japan. The migration of Malabar Muslims to the West Asia has close resemblance to it.

Coastal district of the state sends more migrant to Gulf is just another interesting fact to look at. "The concentration of Gulf migration in Kerala may be linked to its prior-experience in migration and close ties the coastal pockets of the region have always had with the Arab countries. There is incidentally a remarkable coincidence not only in the regional concentration but also in the pattern of Gulf migration to that of the earlier Ceylon, Malaysian migration (Issac 1992: 18). Similar view has been expressed by scholars in the field of study. People in coastal belt also have rich experience and tradition of migration to other countries such as Sri Lanka, Malaysia, Singapore Mauritius and West indies. Trading and matrimonial relationship that Muslims in Kerala maintained with the Arab world for several centuries in the past provided an additional favorable factor for migration (Nair 1982:24). Migration is the outcome of extreme social pressure experienced by the people of Kerala (Vijayan 2004: 07)

Malayalam speaking Mappilas of modern Kerala was a major presence in the maritime trade of Southern India, till late 18th century. They are the descendants of early Arab and Persian traders and sailors who married locally and whose service gained than a niche in local society (Lal: 2007: 34).

Causes and Pattern of the Gulf Migration

Laymen who lived on the breadline found Gulf migration as an exit to come out of the miseries of workless, unwaged and weak living standards. The main reason for migration from Kerala is none other than the economic benefits. Irudaya Rajan et al. (2002) pointed out that through migration, the economic status of the households may improve and their changed lifestyle is the reflection of it. Nair and Pillai (1994) observed that the main cause for migration is the lack of employment opportunities in Kerala. Arabian Gulf was a promising place for many people who voyaged to Gulf in the late sixties and early seventies. In the early days of the oil-boom in the Arab world, people poured to gulf on a larger scale, and it still tells the tale of people went on board ship (Lanchi). Most of the people failed to make a killing and returned with cash and kind just enough to survive and start small business home. There were several expatriates who never returned.

There are several factors that push out people from their birth place. Kerala economy has certain specific unfavorable indicators like high dropping employment, high density of population, downturn in agriculture and dying down industrial sector etc. that put Keralites to migrate. Sufficient facts and figures to show that a significant share of migrants were unemployed prior to migration. Unemployment fell and poverty eased following the flow of foreign money thanks to the gulf migration. Business flourished as remittances encouraged consumption and acquisition of assets, resulting in overall reduction of poverty in Kerala.(Prakash 1998: 209-213). Migration also often has positive consequences for migrants and their communities of origin. People may migrate from areas where there are low-incomes and few opportunities to places where economic growth and innovation present them with new opportunities. Regular remittances, technology and ideas may, under certain circumstances, lead to positive changes in areas of origin.

Push-Pull Factors of the Gulf Migration from Kerala

Scholars hardly find a common ground to form a consensus concerning the causes of migration from Kerala. Broadly, the sum and substance of the temporary labor movement to Gulf from Kerala can be explained by push-pull theory of migration. The phenomenon of migration from Kerala to the Gulf has been accelerated by the two factors mentioned above. There were a number of 'push' factors in the home state to force the people out to any other place for better livelihood. Oil price soared and that in turn helped raise more roads, building and other infrastructure in the Arabian Gulf; copious categories of career opportunities were created with better working conditions. Gulf beckoned thousands of unemployed youths from Kerala as the 'pull' factors attracted their attention. There were leading circumstances to push and pull people from Kerala to the immense opportunities of the Gulf.

Push factors

Various studies have made different postulation to the phenomenon of labor migration from Kerala. According to the various studies of Centre for Development Studies Thiruvananthapuram, the development model followed in Kerala; a vibrant social sector co-existing with a stagnant productive sector (Zacharia 1999: 27), takes the full credit for migration and the progress achieved. By analyzing the process of migration, four important push factors fuelling migration are found in the Kerala model of development. First off, the rapid demographic expansion and the second case is the stagnation in the agriculture. The third element is the accelerated development in the higher education and the final cause the failure of the economic organization in the state to expand employment in the secondary and tertiary sectors (Zacharia 1999: 27).

A study made by Agro-Research centre in Chavakkad village, Thrissur, listed high density of population in the state, shrinking labor absorption in agricultural, sluggish rate of industrial growth and high percentage of education coupled with inadequate employment as the important reasons for the vast exodus towards the Arabian Gulf (AERC1982: 451).

Studies showed another persuasive point which is believed to have pushed people up and away for Gulf destinations. The leading factor was the rising man-land ratio, which touched 7.36 persons per hector land in 1971, being the highest in India. Secondly, sluggish industrial sector failed to provide significant employment opportunity to the people in the state. The high level of education and literacy and the consequent huge backlog of educated unemployed are the third reason (Kurian 2001: 02)

Pull factors

There has been no other region like Gulf that pulled large number of Keralites. Gulf regions pulled people presenting a number of possible opportunities for a better living. Oil boom and opulence went well hand in hand in the Arabian countries. When visas were up for grabs, youth in Kerala saw Gulf as a foreign land full of promises for fulfilling their needs. They were the major pull factors which motivated Keralites to migrate Gulf countries. Choice of a good number of job opportunities, better pay packets, savings etc., are some of the attractive sides that move thousands of fortune seekers to Arab world. For an Indian worker, the core motive for migrating to Gulf is always the substantial wage differential which exists between the two labor markets for the same occupation. The oil price-rise in 1970s and the subsequent employment opportunities in the Gulf resulted a spurt in demand not only for skilled workers, but also semi-skilled and unskilled workers in different fields. The bridge of culture and business was built between Arab world and Kerala earlier than the migration of recent decades apart from the economic factors surfaced above. This in turn contributed very much in the process of Gulf migration from Kerala.

Studies are still mining copious causes of migration to know what always motivates men to move abroad. Hence different studies delve into different reasons of migration. An objective analysis reveals that the factors related to the Kerala model development is economically motivated. As quoted traditionally, push pull factors also have a big role in setting emigrational trend. Over and above, one must also examine other social conditions of the period at the beginning of migration and cultural elements in the community that took part in Migration (Jaleel 2009: 18). To sum up, socio-political conditions of the state and encouraging labor opportunities in the Gulf countries were the two major causes of high volume of migration from Kerala to the oil-rich Arab regions.

Chapter - 5

UPS and Down along the Wave

Muslims in Kerala has been transformed like never before thanks to the local and global factors that set the stage for the changed socio-political life. On that account, the socio-political life of Muslims in Kerala has to be examined within the historical context that contributed to the transformation. A study on Kerala Muslims and their relation to the Arab world and its impacts would be proof less, patchy and partial without analysing the various historical trajectories associated with the community. The firm affair of Kerala Muslims with Arab world also has a unique historical context. It had begun long before the day Islam emerged and flowered in India. But it flourished only after the origin of Islam in Kerala. There is past proof of evidence that the Keralites were the first in India to receive the message of Islam when a group of Muslim Arab traders together with Malik ibn Denar, arrived in Kerala and spread the word of Islam. Since then, Islam has been spreading among the population who were religiously Hindu-based. Today, Muslims are around 24% of the population. They rally behind different religious denominations under the leadership of various religious scholars.

The origin and Growth of Islam in Kerala

As Islam had arrived in Kerala even before it spread out all other places, the Mappila Muslims[1] are the descendants of the first generation Muslims in India. SS Nadvi says "It is an open fact that long before the Muslims settled in Northern India, there were colonies in Southern

India (Nadvi 1934: 478). Hence, two major historical facts reinforce the findings of Nadvi. The first case in a point is the history of Islam which has been associated with global trade and commerce since its early years. And the second fact is Kerala's great maritime trade tradition since time immemorial. The trade relation had been in existence since pre-Islamic period; there was a warm and wooing trade relation between Arabs and Kerala. Inbound and outbound merchandise was shipped between India and Arab world moving various commodities to the ports of Bahrain, Oman, Yemen, and Muscat etc. Arab traders carried those shipments to Hijaz, through land and then to final trade destinations like Egypt and Syria by the Red Sea (Amin 1964:03). Gopal Panikkar observes that the "Long before the origin of Islam, Arabs had planted colonies and their trade establishments all along the Western seaboard of India and especially the Malabar coast" (Panikar 1929: 267).

With extensive costal lines to its pride, Kerala takes advantages as a connecting point in global maritime trade. Warming spices had always attracted foreign merchants to Malabar Coast from very early times. For this reason, Kerala holds an all important position on the trading map of the ancient world. Muzarris was one of the great commercial emporia of the world. It was a meeting place of the East and the West. According to an eminent historian A.P. Ibrahim Kunju, from the very early times, Malabar had a strong maritime trade contacts with west Asian countries. Till the establishment of the Roman Empire[2], the trade monopoly was in the hands of the Arab merchants (Knju 1975:02). Thus, a positive geographical factor was the prime reason for the international exposure of Malabar Coast.

The Arabs were the starting merchants of the Indian Ocean before anybody else could come. They had comfortable and cordial relation with the native rulers in Kerala. Local Hindus welcomed Arabs with open arms. Some of them were domiciled in the major ports and intermarriage was inherent. The trade relation between the Arabs and Kerala played as a vehicle in the spread of Islam in Indian sub-continent and its growth (Hassan 1928: 45). The trade, both coastal and overseas, was dominated mainly by Muslim mercantile communities, though Jews, *Chettis* from Corromandal, and *Vaniyas* from Gujarat all traded in from Calicut and other ports (Kunjali 2004: 92). The frequent reference in ancient sources to trade with the Malabar Coast is impressive. It is in the context of this great traffic of men, merchandise and ideas that we track and trace the origin of the Islam in Kerala.

These Arabs were the ancestors of the Mappila Muslims (Ali 1929:267). Islam spread out in Kerala very early; almost certainly before the end of the 7th Century. There is no direct epigraphic or literary evident to support this date for the origin of Islam in Kerala. The earliest known Muslim who attempted to deal with the subject of Mappila origin was Sheik Ahmed Zein-Ud-din (1498-1581) of Ponnani. He elaborated on the subject in his well-known work "Tuhfat al Mujahideen"- an offering to jihad warriors' which was directed against the Portuguese.

There are a lot of differing observations on the origin and growth of Islam in Kerala. Different scholars have different opinion on the matter. However, discussion of the origin of the Mappilas is incomplete without a fair reference to Cheraman Perumal whose story runs through Kerala's history. Thence, with the process of peaceful communication and economic relationship between Arabia and Kerala, Muslim community in Kerala emerged and flowered shortly after the beginning of Islam itself. The growth of Islam may have received an added encouragement through the conversion of a Malayali ruler. The Arab affinity has affected and continues to affect the language, religion and the culture of the Mappilas more profoundly than those of any other Indian Muslims (Miller 1976: 51).

The Growth of Muslims in Kerala

Soon after the dawn of Islam in Arabia, the faith was widely spread out across the land of Malabar as well. The first eight centuries of Muslim growth following the establishment of Islam in Kerala were marked by an all forward movement (Miller 1976: 51). The count of Arabs in the trading ports as well as the number of who married and settled in these places was steadily on the increase over the centuries. Islam began to disseminate by conversion, immigration and settlement of the Arab traders and others. The early Arab settlements were especially important in the history of Malabar.

The support of the local rulers and the complex social hierarchies among the native Hindu community accelerated the growth of the new faith in Kerala. The principle of universal brotherhood was indeed an attraction to the other castes, mainly men of low caste got converted into Islam, which sequentially helped the Muslim community to a great extent to increase the size of their population in Kerala (Dale 1980). The lower castes who suffered under the existing social order welcomed Islam as an opportunity to secure some degree of social freedom. Even the conversion was supported by the local rulers.

The native rulers such as the Zamorin of Calicut, the Raja of Cochin were very liberal and open hearted in hosting and entertaining the Arabs. They also did everything possible in preaching and promoting Islam in their territories. They encouraged the construction of mosques also. It was the result of a mutual dependency and mutual trust. The native rulers received unequivocal support from the Muslim traders settled down in various parts of Malabar, in turn promoting the reputation as a safe haven for trade; eventually resulted in the economic prosperity of the kingdoms.

Missionary activities also played their role in the growth of the Muslims in Kerala. 'The tradition of Malik Ibn Dinar and his associates who spread the religion of Islam in Kerala is an undeniable fact. To sum up, Muslims had attained a remarkable space in the social life of Malabar at that time. The fourteenth century Arab Travaler, Ibn Batuta[3] revealed that those Muslims had, by the fourteenth century, assembled the institutional and professional infrastructure of an Islamic society (Miller 1967: 51).

The 12th to the 16th century of Mappila history is initially linked with the rise of Zammorin of Calicut (Poonnen 1948:12). There was a notable rapport between Arab, Muslim merchants and Zamorin of Calicut at that period. Economically the coalition had beneficial results for both parties. "The Arabs not only made Calicut the greatest port on the west coast of India but also they even spread the name and fame of the Zamorin to Europe (Ayyer 1938: 52). These were the heavenly days of the Muslim society in Malabar, and thus they kept it up in increasing prosperity right up to the dawn of the 16th century (Ali 1928: 268). In the medieval period the Muslims of Malabar Coast were mainly a trading community and their leadership was in the hands of the Arab merchants or Thangals[4] who had established themselves mainly at Calicut and Cannanore. To sum up, in many ways the political climate has been very favour to Islam to find its existence and flourish for the first eight centuries of the origin of Islam in Kerala. Miller pointed out this fact that 'The growth of Muslims in Kerala in its early years was marked by a calm forward movement. The peaceful contact and development stands in sharp contrast to the progress of Islam in North India' (Miller, 1975: 51).

The Portuguese incursion and Its Impact

At the end of 15th century Portuguese sailors invented the sea route to India from Europe. In 1498 Vasco da Gama with his team of Portuguese traders and missionaries landed at Kappad in Calicut. They thought that it would be very easy to build up a trade relation between Kerala and Europe. Contrary to their expectations they found an extremely unfavourable environment in Malabar. The Arabs were already had a strong friendship with the native rulers of Kerala especially at the various princely states in Malabar. The Hindu Kings had taken the Arabs in to their confidence on trade and the Muslims had a special status in their army.

Not only the Arab Merchants had established a firm and long standing foothold there, but also many of the descendents of the Arabs and the newly converted Muslims were in the service of these Rajas. Kunhali Marakar's position in the naval fleet of Zamorins is the typical example for this cordial relation. The Portuguese could not tolerate the existing circumstances any more. They tried their level best to create intrigues, distrust and rift between the Rajas and Kunjalis intended to weaken the Arab influence and their trade monopoly in the Malabar region. Naturally, the struggle for power led to a vigorous hostility between the Portuguese and Muslims. With the arrival of the Portuguese, Muslims lost their dominance in trade and they withdrew to inlands (Panicker 1981: 96-97)

The political scenario was changed drastically with the arrival of Portuguese. Their arrival in the Indian Ocean in the 15th century backed by imperial arms and savagely destructive tactics evoked a strong response from the Muslims in South India. The constant struggle of Muslims against the colonial invasion adversely affected their political might. It also badly affected the harmony between the native rulers and the Muslim community. The emergence of the Portuguese as a key player in the sea trade and the political domain was a serious setback to the growth of Muslims. Miller says that religiously the Muslims were in a psychological retreat during the Portuguese period. Their dominance along the coast was never restored after the Portuguese period as they turned to inland in search of new livelihoods the Mappilas met outcastes who were in need of change (Miller 1976: 83).

Malabar Rebellion and Aftermath

19th century was an era of furious uprising by the Mappila peasants of Malabar against the upper-hand landlordism of Jenmis on the one hand and Imperialism of the British on the other. These uprisings generally termed by the authorities as Mappila Outrages, varied from small incidents to the major battles and culminated in the rebellion of 1921. They were not mere riots or affrays but murderous outrages such have no parallel in any other her mejesty's dominions. (Minutes by JP Sim, member council of the Governor of Madrass judicial proceedings,no 1606-A,28 August 1874).

The critical period however was from 1836-1853 during which 22 outbreaks registered. During 1829-1921, a total of 51 outbreaks took place. Various theories have been put forward by the experts to explain the root cause of the outbreaks. Rejecting the theory of religious fanaticism fabricated by the British Utilitarions and communalists, liberal and scientific historians had established the economic theory of agrarian discontent. When the imperialists depicted the Mappila rebels as Jungle Mappilas or troublesome race, the national historians called them as Nationalists or revolutionaries. Whatever may be the analysis the fact remains that the outbreaks was the results of the discontent of Mappilas against the oppression of their land lords and the British authorities who supported the landlordism. The philosophical basis of the rebellion was provided by the Muslim religious leaders who declared rebellion against oppression as a meritorious act and death in the attempt as a path to paradise (Logan

1882: 48). The 1921 outbreak was a serious setback in the growth and progress of the Mappila Muslims. Thousands were killed, imprisoned and exiled. The Muslims had to pay big price for the rebellion. The community had lost much of their resources, and confidence above all. The following decades were a tough time for Mappila Muslims in Malabar.

Assertion of Muslim Identity and Institutionalization

Malabar Rebellion and its consequences was a turning point in the history of Kerala Muslims. It redirected and revamped the flow of socio-political life of the community. This was a period when community identity flourished among the Muslims as well as the Hindu community in Malabar. The rebellion became an instrument for making and consolidating community identities. The Khilafat movement which was instrumental in developing a feeling of brethrens to the Muslims in various parts of the world. The pan Islamic sentiment also had given an additional fillip to the emergence of a separate Muslim identity. Muslims also became suspicious of the approach of the congress leadership and began to rethink the structure of the community. Until the outbreak of the Malabar Rebellion, Muslims had not had an organized form of leadership. They were organized and led by some charismatic individual leaders like Variankunnath Kunhahamed Haji, Mamburam Thangal and so on. After the rebellion, Muslim leaders began to think to form a common platform for the Muslims.

The second major political impact of the rebellion was the distrust of the Muslim folks on Congress leadership. "Mappilas were sharing the growing feeling of Indian Muslims that the Congress leadership was not sufficiently sympathetic to Muslim needs and desires" (Miller 1976: 160). The attitude of many Congress leaders led to the alienation of Mappilas from the Congress movement. Gradually, Muslims began to give away their faith in congress and Muslim League came forward to influence them. In short, the lesson they learned from Malabar Rebellion and its impact led to form two form of organized wing for the Muslims, the first movement was 'Muslim Aykyasangam' and the other one was Muslim League.

Muslim Aikya Sangam was the first deliberate attempt to organize the Muslims in Kerala with a modern outlook. It had to fight for a renaissance in the Muslim community. The organization paved the way for the formation of two pivotal organizations for the Muslims in the state- Muslim league and Kerala Nadvathul Mujahideen. These two organizations, like other movements, played an unequivocal role in the identity formation of Kerala Muslims. It has been argued that the Muslim league was the natural continuation of the Muslim Aikya Sangham, particularly as K.M.Seethi Saheb and K.M.Moulavi who were involved in the formation of the Aikya Sangham were involved in founding Muslim League also.

Muslim Aikya Sangam

The catastrophic experience of Malabar Rebellion influenced the educated sections of Muslims to think about a solution to overcome the pathetic situation and save the community from the stalemate. They realised that only through organized efforts, not through individual initiatives, they could chalk out a programme for improvement of the community. Muslim Aikya Sangam was the result of such kinds of discussion and deliberation in the Muslim intelligentsia at the post Malabar rebellion scenario. Though the deliberation of the formation of an organisation for Muslims had started before the Malabar Rebellion, it gained momentum in the post rebellion period. The disputes between leading Muslim families in Kodungallur was also instrumental for the formation of Aikya Sangam.

In this background, a group of visionary Muslim leaders and scholars gathered at Eriyad (Kodungallur[5]) in 1922, to discuss the issues and challenges of Muslim community in Kerala and to form an organization to address their grievances. They formed an organisation called '*Nishpaksha Sangam*', and its immediate attention to settle the disputes among Muslim families of Kodungallur. The meeting was presided over by Hamadani Thangal, who urged Muslims about the need for an organised movement and to form a broad organization to tackle more issues related to Muslims in Kerala. At the*gam* convened its first meeting at Eriyad in 1922 itself and decided to expand its activities and renamed it as *MuslimAikya Sangam* (Maulavi

1960: 470). Thus, the first Muslim organization representing the Muslims of Malabar, Cochin and Travancore was set up in 1922.

Religious denomination and its Activities

Muslim community in Kerala is not a single religious entity. There are a number of groups and streams with difference of opinion on various matters to religious and cultural life. The Muslims in Kerala, who form roughly a fourth of the state's population, are broadly divided into three broad groups, each being what could be called a separate Islamic interpretative community based on differences in the understanding and interpretation of Islam. The largest in terms of numbers are *Sunnis* (Yoginder)[6]. The other two broad groups among the Kerala Muslims are the *Jamaat-e-Islami* and the *Kerala Nadwathul Mujahidin*. The differences of opinion on various issues related to preach and practice of the religion led to develop a number of approaches and schools among the Muslims in the state by the time. Difference of opinion proves to be a fact that the community of faith is intellectually alive, that it posses religious passion and, that it wants to both to conserve the past and faithfully move in to the future. All these differences are not positive and tolerant. Some of them led to deep division, grave rivalry and further organizational division.

Islahi/Mujahid Movement

Islahi movement (Salafi movement) was an organizational extension of the Muslim Aikya Sangam. *Kerala Jam-Iyyathul Ulama* which was established in 1924 in Aluway, Kerala, under the leadership of K.M. Mawlawi, M.C.C Abd al-Rahman Mawlawi and E.K. Mawlawi was the frontrunner of the Mujahid Movement in Kerala. Their pivotal motive of the KJU was to purify the Muslim society from superstitions and innovations in religion. The organization was formed when these scholars felt that Kerala Muslim *Aykya Sangam*, an organization formed in 1922, for promoting unity among the Muslims of Kerala, was not enough to propagate their ideas (Maulavi 1997: 09). They started working together in Kerala Muslim society until the discharge of the *Aykya Sangam* in 1934.

The ideological background of the organization was the revivalist thought of the Egyptian Salafi stream led by the scholars such as Jamal din Afghani, Muhammed Abdu and Rashid Rida. They were not influenced by the *Gulf Salafism* initiated by Muĺammed ibn Abd al-Wahhab in Najd which is the mainstream movement in today's Saudi Arabia. One of the *Islahi* scholars of Kerala, Muĺammed Ali Sullami states that the scholars like Jamal al-Din al-Afghani, Rashid Rida and Muhammad Abduh, influenced the *Islahi* Movement in Kerala just like other countries in the world. The trend of Muslim society all over the world changed because of their contributions in the academic and educational fields. Kerala was also very much influenced by their thoughts and views. But, it is not so in the Gulf countries (Sullami 2002: 22-23).

The founding leaders of the Muslim Aikya Sanhgam and the KJU were inspired by the works of the Egyptian *salafi* scholars. Their views were propagated in their official magazine called '*al-Manar*'. It dealt with various issues among the Muslim society, providing scholarly as well as a revolutionary themes to their writing. These copies reached the hands of certain scholars in Kerala who became motivated by its philosophies and world view. Later, the Mujahid movement started publishing a magazine to propagate their ideas with the same name "*al-Manar*".

KJU was strongly opposed to much of the customs and practices prevailed in Muslim community at that time. They opposed all forms of customs like *nerchas, Chandanakudam, Moulud, Ratib*, in the religious practice of Muslims. They described it as *Bidath,* must be avoided and abandoned since it is contrary to the original teachings of Islam (Kutty 1978: 439-51). The reformist scholars launched uncompromising course of campaign against traditional Ulamas and Musliyars. It is not surprising that the internecine politics among the Ulamas became central to the social transactions among the Muslims. While majority among Muslims accepted the traditional Sunni faith, a revisionist purist tradition also appeared which was formalized into an organization named Kerala Nadwathul Mujahideen in 1950.

Kerala Nadwathul Mujahideen

Today, Mujahid movement is also known as *Salafi* Movement or *Islahi* Movement, around Islamic circles in Kerala. The primary objective of the organization is believed to be spreading the message of Islam based on monotheism. The next major concern was eradication of social evils like dowry system and superstitious beliefs. Another core area of attention of Mujahid movement was promotion of religious as well as modern education and undertaking humanitarian works. In this way, the formational motive of the Islahi movement in Kerala was stated to be a revival movement like the tradition of Egyptian Salafi movments.

Today, there are various feeder organizations under the umbrella of Kerala Nadwathul Mujahideen including their Ulama Council Kerala Jamiyyatul Ulama. *Ittihadul Shubbanul Mujahideen* (ISM) is their youth wing formed in 1966, with a view to lead the youth of Kerala in the light of the Quran. ISM has currently become one of the most active Islamic youth movements in Kerala. Its work ranges from Islamic *dawah (preach)* to humanitarian activities like free medical camps, educational support and campaigns against terrorism etc. *Mujahid* Students' Movement (MSM) is the student wing of Kerala *Nadwathul Mujahidin*, was formed in 1971. MSM's chief objective was stated to propagate Islamic ideals and principles among the student community in campuses and schools. Mujahid Girls Movement (MGM) is the girls and women's wing of KNM. At first, the girls were organized under the banner of MSM girls' wing. Later, to enable larger participation and convenient functioning, a separate ladies wing of KNM namely MGM was organized in 1987. MGM encourages Muslim women to promote Islamic values among themselves. Study classes and family gatherings are arranged to impart Islamic knowledge

Contributions of *Nadwathul Mujahidhin*

The contribution of Kerala Nadwat Ul-Mujahidhin is very clear in the religious as well as the social life of the Muslims in Kerala. Salafi Scholars took a strong standpoint against the system of dowry and the practice of triple *Talaq*. They gave the fatwa that triple *Talaq*, the practice of saying divorce thrice at once, is not recognized by Islam. That was contrary to what was practiced by the conservatives who opined that triple *Talaq* is permissible. Islahi movement initiated the practice of delivering the *khutubah* (Friday Prayer) in Malayalam for the first time. In the past, Friday sermon was given in Arabic language everywhere in Kerala. KNM was the first to translate the Quran in to Malayalam with commentary. They were also the first Muslim organization in Kerala to give permission to women to pray in masjid and encouraged them to pray in a separate women's prayer room inside the mosque. All these were often against the prevailing practices adopted by the conservative Muslim scholars of Kerala.

KNM has played a key role in the empowerment of Muslim women in Kerala with its revolutionary policies within the religious and social circle. They gave great importance for women education. Islahi movement was the driving force behind the setting up of Muslim educational institutions in Kerala. They encouraged men and women to acquire modern education which helped transform many places of Malabar region into highly educated areas. They have also initiated a modern Madrasa system in the state to cater to the religious educational needs of boys and girls, and formalized the religious education system. They also established a number of Arabic colleges which offer B.A *Afsal al-Ulama*[7] courses. Some of them are affiliated to the University of Calicut while others to the University of Kannur. A number of Arts, Science, Technical and private colleges were also established later.

Splits and Rifts

Difference of opinion among the scholars on religious matters has resulted in splits within the KNM. There are around six streams within Islahi sect in the state. But there have been three major partitions within the organization in the last two decades. The first major split occurred when Hussayn Madawur, a prominent Salafi scholar of Kerala decided to form a separate group as a result of the difference of opinion to the existing leadership of the Kerala Nadvathul Mujahideen. This split was in 2006 and the splinter party is known as Madawur group. This split was attributed to a deviation in '*manhaj*', as they described it as the deviation from the real '*manhaj of salaf*'. There were also rumors of some financial issues that came up within the organization that led to the split.(Lakkal 2006: 16). At the end, these two groups reunited in December 2016, to go hand in hand and work together.

Another major split came to pass in 2009, when Zubayr Mankada, another prominent scholar, started his own organization saying the current *Islahi* movement was rooted in *bidah*. His followers today practice a form of living that is closely adjusted to the conditions the times of the Prophet of Islam. Withdrawn from the society, they lead a reclusive lifestyle. Since they began to migrate to Yemen to lead a spiritual life like the prophet, the group is also called Dammaj Salafis. *Jinnu* group led by two salafi scholars namely Zakariyya Swalahi and Mujahid Balusseri, is just another faction. Thus, while KNM, the mother organization still exists, all the offshoot sects go with their own mission and method to propagate their views in Kerala.

Samastha Kerala Jam-iyyathul Ulama

Even though the Aikya Sangam gained much popularity among Muslim intelligentsia, it was not able to attract the attention of the Muslim masses in Kerala. The traditionalist opposition grew in intensity when their religious leaders came under sharp criticism from the reformists scholars. Orthodox Muslim leaders got cheerful support from Muslims at the grassroots who were the lion share of the Muslim population at that time. Perhaps, it was the adamant stand of reformists against popular beliefs and practices of Muslims, which invited vehement opposition from the traditionalist *Ulama*. They were disturbed by the ongoing modernisation trends in Western style, and in the first public circulation among Kerala Muslims of fundamentalist and puritanical views of Muhammed bin Abdul Wahab (1702-1793), Salafism of Rashid Rida (1865-1935) Islamic modernism of Muhammed Abduh(1819-1905), pan Islamism of Jamaluddin Afghani (1839-1897) (Faizy 2012: 928)

The social base of the reformist scholars, most of them from middle class background was also a factor behind their failure in the rural Malabar. Above all, the lion share of traditional scholars and their followers were suspicious on the entire activities of the Aikya sangam leaders. They strongly believed that the new ideas and suggestions which promoted by the reformist leaders an aberration from the right path of the Islamic tradition as well as the divine scripture of the holy Quran and teaching of the prophet. Moulana Pangil Ahmed Kutty Musliyar who had already started a counter campaign against the

'Wahabi ideology' met renowned religious scholar Varakkal mullakkoya thangal to discuss the need of an organisational movement to defend the 'true spirit' of the religion. Thangal suggested convening a meeting of the eminent scholars to discuss the suitable solution.

In 1925, the orthodox Muslim scholars met at Kuttichira Juma Masjid and formed a parallel organisation called *Kerala Jam-iyathul Ulama.* Pangil Ahammad Kutty Musaliyar and Varakkal Mulla Koya Thangal were the founding leaders of the new organisation. On 26th June in 1926, a convention of *Kerala Jam-iyathul Ulama* was held at Calicut Town Hall and the organization was renamed as *Samastha Kerala Jam-iyathul Ulama (*All Kerala Ulama Organisation. *The* formation of Samastha was the response of the traditional Ulama to the condition of post 1921 period in which Kerala Muslim community generally witnessed a radical shift from the fold of individual leadership to the fold of organisations (Faizy 2012: 928).

The organisation was registered on 14th November 1934, with a forty-member committee (*Mushavara*). The social structure of the Muslims in Rural Malabar was fertile land for the growth of *SKJU*, because of the hegemony of the traditional Ulama on every sphere of their social life. In short, within a decade itself, *SKJU* could line up Muslim masses under their banner. The leaders of Samastha travelled throughout the state to convey the message of the Ulama organisation to maximum religious scholars who were living in the mosques and religious educational centres serving Islamic knowledge. According to the bylaw, the main aim of the organisation is propagation of true Islam. Encouragement of secular education compatible with religious beliefs is also its objective.

The Organisational Structure

Mushavara, which consists of forty eminent scholars, is the supreme body of Samastha. The word Mushavara, which means consultation, is drawn from the Quranic scripture to seek scholarly advice. Later Samastha formed a fatwa committee within the Mushavara to specially look in to the increasing queries on religious issues. Sunni Yuvajana sangam (SYS), the youth wing of Samastha, was formed at the 20th annual conference held at Tanur on 25th April 1954, to organize

Muslim youth under Samastha banner. Came into being on 19th February 1989, as part of their attempt to put Muslim students together under its folder, the student wing, Samastha Kerala Sunni Student Federation (SKSSF), was yet another milestone in the history of Samastha. Other major feeder organizations of Samastha Kerala Jam'Eyyath Ul Ulama, are Samastha Kerala Sunni Balavedi, Samastha Kerala Muslim Employees Association and Madrassa management Association.

Madrasa Education

In the wake of big shift in educational landscape and unfavourable regulatory frameworks for functioning of elementary schools and Othupallis together, Muslim leaders and Ulamas became concerned about the future of religious education. As a consequence, Madrasa education got restructured into formal model of education. The situation paved the way for a separate body to run and regulate the religious education. Thus Samastha Kerala Islam Matha Vidyabhasa Board (SKIMVB) was formed in March 1951.

Samastha Kerala Islam Matha Vidhyabhyasa Board is the powerful central body of Madrasa under the organization. It was formed in the 19th annual conference at Vatakara to meet the urgent need for a centralized Madrasa system. There were only ten applications for approval when the board called for madrasa registration at first time in 1952. The number of registered and recognized moral schools (Madrasa) has been on an amazing increase since then. By March 2011, the number of moral schools (Madrasa) registered with and recognized by Samastha was 9015. All the moral schools (Madrasa) have classes at least up to fifth grade. There are 4886 moral schools (Madrasa) with grades up to 7th and 1493 with grades up to 10th and 312 with standards up to 12th class.

Under the parent organization Samastha, Sunni Mahallu Federation is the apex body of the Mahallu. The dynamic context, in which an average Muslims lived, was defined by the course of activities the organization pursued. Samastha initially concentrated on three areas and worked on a series of programme accordingly. Building and renovation of masjids, which would be religious and cultural centre for Muslims was the top priority. The second was the establishment of Yatheem Khanas (Orphanages), which they believed, would provide refuge for orphans and destitute families in the community. From Islamic perspective too, they found it was an obvious answer to the problem of destitution and misery of the ordinary Mappila, which would counteract an insurgent or even a possible revolutionary disposition. And the third was the promotion of Madras education. The spiritual leadership under Samastha developed a variety of educational system to impart Islamic knowledge to each and every section of the society in a way best suited to and compatible with their period. There were Othupalli for primary education, and for higher education, dars in masjid. Towards a contemporary society, Samastha came up with the daily 'Suprabhatham'. Besides the daily, six periodicals are published. Yet another new turn to change educational landscape into infotainment with changing times, Darsana TV was launched laudably under the leadership of Samastha Kerala Jamiyathul Ulama.

The Three Splits

The history of Samasta, the larger and powerful body of Sunnis in Kerala, is incomplete without the sorry story of partition. The organization split three times. In 1966, when Samasta described Tablighi Jama'at as anti Islamic; the first crack-apart was of the kind. Walking out, under the leadership of Sheik Hassan Hazarath and K.C, and Muhammed Maulavi Pangil, the splinter group lined up under a new banned named Akhila Kerala Jami'at al Ulama. Another shock came as the use of loud speaker in Friday Khutba, became a bone of contention. A parallel organization called Samasta Kerala Jamiat al Ulama came into existence by the Ulama, who opposed the use of loud speaker in Masjid formed. Both these splits did not much affect the regular business of Samasta. In 1989, when Kanthapuram A.P. Abubaker Musliyar, walked out with his followers, the third and major earthquake of separation shook Samasta. Split into two, a splinter group AP sunni led by Kanthapuram A.P. Abubaker Musliyar and the other groups called as EK Sunni, Samastha was no longer a single force. Both groups had no deep ideological differences. However, they maintained a different ground for politics and some religious aspected.

Jamaate Islami Hind

In 1941, the history of Indian Muslim took yet another course of journey as Abul A'la Moududi, founded a pan India Islamic movement called Jamaate Islami Hind. Through their pamphlets and journals put in circulation by the disciples in Kerala, Moududian thoughts were familiar to Malabar Muslims by 1930's itself. A group of religious scholars were influenced by the ideology of Maududi through his Urdu publication Tharjumanul Quran (Hameed 2014: 512). His perspectives, perceptions and practices were popular among Urdu scholars.

Inspired by the new school of Islamic thought, V.P. Mohamed Ali and K.M. Moulavi, were the earliest advocates of the group in Malabar. K.M. Moulavi translated Moududi's works and published it in Al-Murshid. This was instrumental for Maududian thoughts among the Islahi followers in Kerala. Mohammed Ali along with Issudhin Sahib, brought into being a new organization called 'Jamaiyathul Mustarshidin', with a forty member committee at Valancheri in 1948 (Abdurahuman 1992:241). Later, it was converted in to the first unit of Jamate Islami in Malabar. In a short space of time, a number of branches of the organization were set up in various parts of Malabar. In 1948 August, the leaders of this group met in Calicut and formed a central committee called 'Shura' (Abdurahuman 1992:241) A resolution to publish an official mouthpiece '*Prabhodanam*', was passed in the meeting.

Going arm in arm with mutual understanding and better cooperation and in some cases with common agenda related to social life of the Muslims, Jamaat and KJU found many grounds to go together in the early days. Unfortunately, the honeymoon between the KJU and Jama'th did not last. As back as 1950's itself, a group of scholars including K.M. Moulavi, issued a combined fatwa against Jamate Islami (Moidumoulavi 1992: 125). Despite its disagreement on Thagooth, any form of government, including democracy, Islamic or non-Islamic, which governs people without heeding the commandment of the god, Mujahid groups were somewhat soft-minded about the ideals of Jamaat. In the run up to the first Parliament election held in 1951, Jamate Islami insisted its members to abstain from electoral activities (Laith 1951: 28).

The political position of Jamaat to stand out was not digestive to many Muslims in Kerala. And it was welcomed by neither Sunnis nor Mujahids in Kerala. As if found a common ground despite being arch rivals, both became the staunch critics of Jamaate Islami since 1950's. Among other mainstream movements, contributing considerably for cultural and social uplift of Muslim community, JIH Kerala has been maintaining its stand alone identity since those days. A host of services like building mosques wherever needed, giving guidelines and support for the effective running of the existing masjids, arranging training sessions for Imams and Qatibs, setting up arrangements for Zakat, Fithir Zakat, Sacrifices, breaking of fast in each Mahal (Local Muslim community affiliated to a masjid) are the routine services of Kerala Masjid Council, set up by JIH with a purpose.

The Impact of Institutionalization

Being a place of worship as well as center for cultural involvement, a Masjid is a peaceful place away from home as far as Muslim community is concerned. The practice of raising masjid in various parts of the state found as back as the day Islam emerged. Muslim religious educational institutions also might have started from the early days of Islam in Kerala. Masjids where students attended for Islamic lessons served as religious educational institutions too. Education, during the pre-colonial, was put first by the community. The big-hearted support of well to do members of the community was the lifeblood for every day management of masjid. Top priority for education was the on the top in the wish list of Muslim leaders in their mission for a reformed society. On the other hand, they always gave preference for setting up of institutions for imparting religious education. The institutions functioned without any fiancé or facilities from local and state administration.

Early days of religious schooling took students to Othupallis or Makthaps; a single teacher primary schools for fundamentals of religious education. Othupallies were there in every nook and corner where a large Muslim population had been living. Teaching fundamentals, the institutions had every day dose of Islamic lessons for attendees. Moulavi or Mullah was the teacher who was in charge of the masjid which did double duty of education and worship. Though there were a number of Othupallies in Kerala, none of it followed any kind of rule and regulations. It was an armature set up in its functioning.

For higher education on religious matters, the students used to go to Madrassas or Palli Dars[8] which were usually attached with the mosques. Under the supervision of imam or any other religious scholars who have traditional knowledge in Quran and Fiqh, Dars functioned well every day. Muslim community in respective Mahallus volunteered themselves with support in cash and kind to support the education. Rich people in the Mahallus were used to bearing the cost of running Dars. In many places, each and every member in the community had to put aside something from their earnings for the educational purpose. It was mandatory as well as Mahallu authorities were compelled to give their dues. Course of instructions were as different as chalk and cheese from Madrasa to Madrasa, which led the students learning Islamic moral lessons from Madrasa to Madrasa and from place to place throughout the country.

Though there is always an internal disagreement on the matters related to customs, belief and the very approach to the socio-political issues, all sects of the Muslim movement have played a crucial role in redefining and reshaping the religious landscape of Muslims in Malabar. The reformists as well as the orthodox movements has brought about a fresh awareness among the ordinary Muslims and as an inevitable result, helped transform followers into a community full of life. Its role and characters have been changed in different period. All these organizations in their own way contributed to the growth of the community consciousness among the Mappilas of Malabar. With a competitive spirit, they started new educational and welfare institutions, published umpteen literatures on various issues related to the society in general and the social life of Muslims in particular.

Muslim religious organizations in Kerala are entirely different from the like-minded organizations in the various parts of the country. The major component of this specialty is nothing but the years-long interaction with the Arab world. Each and every movement in the

Arab Islamic world has had its impact on the functioning of the various Muslim religious organizations in Kerala. The influence of the Arab world has altered their policy and programs time by time. All these organizations have their feeder organizations in every settlement in the Gulf countries. These organizations are the lifeline of the regular course of religious activities.

Notes

1. The term *Mappila* is cited in different forms in different sources of literature as 'Mappila', 'Mappilla', and 'Moplah'.This study has referred 'Mappila" throughout the chapters.
2. Roman Empire means the empire established by Augustus in 27 BC and divided by Theodosius in 395CE intothe Western or Latin and Eastern or Greek Empires.
3. Muhammad Ibn Battuta was a Moroccan scholar who widely travelled the medieval world. He arrived in India in 1333.
4. "*Thangals*" are the descendants of the prophet Muhammed who came from the deferent parts of Arabia and settled in Kerala. They have been a highly respected segment of the society and were honoured. Their ancestors claimed to be from the Prophet's family.
5. Kodungallur was one of the few Muslim pockets in Kerala, where there was a wealthy and educated Muslim intelligentia.
6. Sikand, Yoginder, Traditional' Ulama And 'Modern'Islamic Education In Kerala Countercurrents.org
7. Afsal al-Ulama is an equivalent course to B.A. Arabic in India.
8. Dars are higher education institutions for Muslims to impart religious education which are usually attached with the mosques. Higher education was imparted through the supervision of Imams.

Chapter - 6

Sea of Changes

Unlike other states in India, Kerala stands out with a unique socio-religious structure. Of the 3.5 Crore population, both Muslim and Christian community come 40%. Besides, there are two districts where these two communities dominate. Malappuram a district with the largest poulation, has 70% Muslim population. Pathanamthitta, having the least population is a Christian majority district (Zakariah 2016:31). The deep influence both international and domestic migration has incontrovertibly inspired the socio-economic-political life of people in the state. Perhaps, the migration inspired the way the history of these two major communties composed. From south districts to north tribal highlands, Chrisrians spread their presence. This defined the direction of the community's population progress. The socio-political life of Christian community was boosted at the end half of 20th century when skilled labours moved to Europe and American continents (Benyamin 200: 98). Meanwhile, gulf migration in 1970 gave a life-changing momentum for Muslim community in Kerala (Zakariah 2016:18). The entry of unskilled workers into gulf destinations had critical impact. Expatriates remitted money which helped Kerala form a different socio-economic-political settings against the rest of the states in India. A new trend setting flow of population searching a favouring fortune lifted Muslim community in a considerable way.

Kerala pictured a comparatively improved life of Indian Muslim minority in Post-independent India. The collective social development index and stand alone social scene of Kerala unlike other states in

India, set the stage for an upward growth of Muslim community. Though there is an apparent social, regional imbalance in resource allocation, Kerala presented an inclusive growth model. As a major minority community Muslims forming 24 per cent are represented duly in the growth graph of the state. In brief, Muslims and the geographic areas covering them are part of the progress report the state presented following the signature Kerala development model. A fair and square public wealth allocation and policy work-out consecutive secular governments executed with a great alert helped backward Muslim community catch up with other forwarders. Certainly, a progressive political perspectives and communal harmony the state shared too moved Muslims to the socio-economic-political front.

A microscopic analysis factoring all these will reveal how gulf migration and its multi-directional influence made Kerala Muslims especially Malabar Muslims a privilege-community in forming socio-economic-political-cultural opinion of the state. Even if the community is credited with strong socio-political backing to come to the fore, the significant side of top-to-toe social change is the result of migration-powered progress. Their life took to a whole new level rather than limiting the change into financial prosperity and self-reliance. Economic prosperity infected other life areas too. Financial self-reliance gave them with a powerful political position. The upped living index altered the way Muslims connected socially and perceived social life. Expatriates sending regular money created a huge leap in education and renewed spirit in cultural life. Above all, the community is still under the religious, spiritual sedation gulf migration caused. Over four and a half decade in the past, different organized Muslim movements developed new form and working strategy. Following the migratory process, there have been undesirable trends and tendencies endangering the strong social connect and cultural exchanges. This chapter introduces multiple areas where migratory process has deep influence.

Economic self-reliance and gulf migration

Most men moved to gulf job destinations to find a favourable fortune are from Kerala. According to the statistics in 2014 (CDS 2014), around 24, 00, 575 lakhs Malayalis live and work in seven gulf countries (Zakaria 2015: 05). Interestingly, the routine remittances from these expatriates sustain the state's economy. Around Rs 71, 142 Cr. Kerala received from expatriates in 2014. That is 36.3% of the Net Domestic Product (NSDP) of the state. More men flocked to gulf are from four districts in Malabar- Kozhikkode, Kasargode, Kannur and Malappuram. Of all the religions, Muslims made the most of the migratory process since oil boom in 1970. In the three focal villages this study centered, 92 per cent families have at least one bread winner in gulf. 54 per cent families have more than one member employed abroad. Eight families settled in gulf with their family and visit only once every two years, shared their expatriate-experience during this research visit.

According to the latest statistics produced by the Centre for Development Studies, Thiruvananthapuram, Muslims in Gulf sent Rs 25,767 cr to home in (Zakaria 2015: 21). Muslims make 36.2 per cent of the total gulf remittances. On an average, a Muslim family receives Rs 1,44,000/ a year from Non-Resident Indian (NRI) family members working abroad. Nevertheless falling below in per capita income, given the full volume of fund inflow, Muslims are far ahead. Lion share of the hard-earned money to families from working expatriates goes to Malappuram and Kozhikkode. 4,55, 696 gulf expatriates hail from Malappuram. Kzhikkode (2,26, 499). Kannur (2,91, 321). Muslim expatriates constitute 41.3 per cent. 92.6 per cent of them live in gulf. Out of 100 Muslim households, 60% has men working in gulf countries. Among Hindu households the rate is 18%-19%. Malappuram leads the trend with 35.8% expatriates among the community (Zakaria 2015:21). Since Muslim community has the comparative advantage of more men working outside India, the same reflects their financial progress too. In short, Gulf migration has given the community financial upper hand over the rest of the communities. Muslim households received Rs 25,767 crore or 36.2% of the total remittances in 2014. Hindus received Rs 28,137 crore or 39.6% of the total and the Christian community received Rs 17,238 crore or 24.2%.

The three demographic locations under the study are the beneficiaries of remittances through money exchanges in Gulf.

However, the probe through both survey and private conversation has failed to figure out the exact quantity of fund a household receives a year. However, there is an accurate account of where much of the money gets drained to. A large chunk of gulf money is put in property development, home construction, consumer durables, education, religious and philanthropic missions etc. CDS study confirms that the whole state of Kerala follows the spending fashion.

Remittances are spent on daily household consumption, consumer durables, construction, repair of building, acquisition of lands, education and religious ceremonies. (Zachariah, Rajan 2012: 48). K C Zachariah writes that Kerala's household characterised by a wide range of consumer goods and high consumption levels. Foreign goods have become wide spread and are deemed as a necessity to maintain basic status in the society. There is a general argument that Kerala society has shifted its orientation to consumerism as a result of Gulf migration. Importantly Kerala's social and cultural landscape is highly influenced by migratory process and remittances. Foreign goods have become wide spread and are deemed as a necessity to maintain basic status in the society .As inbound flights grew over decades, purchasing power boosted among the general public. Luxury homes popped up, roads flooded with ritzy cars, wardrobes changed. By 90's there was a retrending and more money spent on education. Go to places like Nadapuram and Kasargode for more visual evidence.

Migrants-sending-money is the spine sustaining god's own country's economy. Evidently, Rs 71,142 cr flowed into Kerala in 2014. That is 36.3% of the state's Net Domestic Product (Mani 2006: 48). Having unfelt any credit crisis or financial meltdown, Kerala has maintained a steady growth rate thanks to the oil money. Job markets and business streets in Kerala are still hustling and bustling owing to one main factor that expatriates send foreign money home on end. The personal finance and state development plans are drawn up with high hopes in an uninterrupted finance inflow from Gulf States. Every term, ruling governments take advantages of the foreign money flow. Islamic banking was the centerpiece of budget discussion in 2014. The then finance minister Dr Thomas Issac came up with a dream proposal to arrange fund streamlining small deposits from expatriates through Islamic banking.

No wonder why every nook and cranny in Kerala is inviting with Automatic Teller Machines and branches of all major bankers in India. These bankers operate across the length and breadth of Kerala to explore huge chunk of money expatriates remit from Gulf States. Both nationalized and private banks open branches widely to explore their fair share of banking business. Gulf migration sped up urbanization in a great way. Even in small towns too, there are duty free outlets selling household electronics to cosmetics imported from gulf countries. Gradually, sleepy villages metamorphosed into urban areas. Better living standards developed even in remote places as migration helped village bread winners put better food on the table. The contribution expatriates have given for reviving the state is commendable.

Changed dynamics of Muslim movements

The idea of organization was firstly introduced in Kerala by Muslims. Although Muslims were not organized under religious leaders till nineteenth centuary, they were organized as a society (Pokker 2013:73). The organization of Muslims caused to understand the importance of organization to the Keralates (Ganesh 1990: 256). In 1980's, Muslim organized movements showed a phase of significant growth. It was a time characterized by complete control of religious organizations over believers and hownes of faith. Institutionalized religious groups excercised excessive reign over faithful followers. Oil-boom-inspired migration came to phase two and positive employment prospects were well utilized. It was then when Malayalis swelled in numbers in gulf. The second phase created more avenues for religious movements too. They reaped the benefits of the boon migration during the phase.

As a result, a little portion of money most Muslim households received went to the running of the religious organizations and their missionary work. Till then, the operational expenses of the organizations were funded by way of the tiny payments landlords made from their agro-revenues. Muslim migration to gulf destinations changed all these systems. Labours sweating their blood under the blazing sun in the desert then were able to subscribe more money than local landlords. Gulf money played a big role in the life of Mappilas. The gap between rich and poor appeared and the middle class Mappila became more powerful. Money made the confidence of Malabar Muslims high. More charity works taken place at Malabar after gulf migration (Miller 1997: 309). Sense of social commitment developed as a result of the privilege expatriate status moved he common-men-turned-moneyed-non-residents to liberally contribute to the social work of religious institutions. This source of finance created a more disciplined work culture among religious organizations.

Not only NRK's but also employers in gulf countries knowingly or unknowingly became a part of religious institutions and their functioning. Jump in oil revenue boosted gulf economy every which way. Gulf economies made a huge progress in trade and commerce. Citizens of those countries grew richer in a short pace time. The share of Zakath payable out of the swollen wealth reached the poor globally. Keralites skillfully routed the resources Arabs earmarked for philanthropy into every nook and cranny of Kerala. Villages in Kerala turned out to be concrete jungles. And cities glass jungles. Meanwhile, more and more Masjids and Madrasas came up in rural Kerala thanks to the charity Arabs earmarked in the blood-finance purifying process observed with a religious perspective. Muslims in Kerala owe a debt of gratitude to Arab citizens for allocating a fair chunk of their aid for reviving religious movements. It's no surprise that 80 per cent of the religious-purpose property development received liberal support from Arab world. Apart from Masjids and Madrasas, they have also extended generous support to develop schools, hospitals, libraries and many other socio-cultural institutions across Kerala.

Rulers of GCC states have also given big help to raise and run socio-cultural institutions under various religious factions. A share of their soveriegn wealth oil boom generated is set aside for missionary activities and humanitarian mission globally. Most underprivileged Muslim worlds received the fund from Arabs. A large portion of the fund flowed to Kerala too. Religious leaders and bureaucrats from Kerala in different gulf government departments actively worked to fetch home the welfare fund Arabs appropriated for philanthropy. Most early migrants secured entry permit through their close friend and relatives who had already made it there. It was when migration phase two came, religious institutions joined the club. Even in Friday sermons, there were words to support the poor with work permit in gulf. AP faction leveraged their network in UAE for recruting men there while Mujahid group and Jamate Islami recruited men to Saudi Arabia and Qatar respectively (Benyamin 2017: 98).

Mujahid factions have inside track in Saudi regime. *Jamate Islami*'s inside influence is in Qatar regime and Sunni AP factions network in UAE has helped them very much to seek to Gulf Rulers attention towards their missionary activities. Pro *Salafi* administration in Saudi Arabia gives a great deal of support for the spread of *Salafism*. The financial aid from Saudi Arabia was used to invigorate *Salafi* movement in the state. Cost of operating *Masjids* and Madrasas met with the fund. Besides, *Mujahid* movement's official magazines and news paper launched and operational overhead met with the monetary assistance. *Jamate Islami* deepened its inside influence in Qatar regime getting its stalwarts placed in public offices. Today, *Jamate Islami* has its people placed in critical places in Qatar and elsewhere in gulf states.

Much debated, the most recent political development in GCC states is a case in a point to prove it. Saudi Arabia and its allies closed borders blocking Qatar from all sides. A complete embargo came in to effect. Muslim religious groups seemed divided on the move Saudi and its allies made. *Jamate Islami* and its branch organizations strongly opposed the siege Saudia Arabia and its allies put against Qatar. However, the wrath the organization shared hasn't reflected in their press opinion. The media they managed consciously quietened on the issue. They feared that any media position against Saudi Arabia-led move seeking a border block on Qatar would negatively affect their media operation in countries like UAE, Bahrain, Saudi Arabia and Kuwait. *Jamate Islami* based its strategic position putting its media operation first. On the complete contrary, *Mujahid* factions stood by Saudi Arabia's move. In a way or other ideological interests of GCC states are deep-rooted in the views Kerala Muslim organizations share.

From Egyptian Salafism to Saudi Salafism- the big stake of migration in Muslim renainssance in Kerala

Islam had arrived India since the period of prophet Muhammad. There are earlier references to the Muslims in Malabar in the notes of Arab travelers and geographers (Miller 1976: 51). The tradition of Malik Ibn Dinar is considered as the first missionary activity in the spread of Islam in Kerala (Kunju, 1995: 24). In fact, Islam first entered India through Kerala's coast. Kerala has a significance to receive Malik Bin Dinar and his message of Islam. Trade treaty prevailed that time boosted the spread of Islam in the State. Today, Kerala has 24 per cent Muslim population. Sufism-inspired Muslim life could get on well with the cultural frontiers of Kerala. In Muslim social life of 14 centuries, *Salfism* is comparatively a young phenomenon. It was only in the first spell of 20th century, *Salafism* found its influence in Muslim views.

Entered officially in 1924, *Jam Iyyatul Ulama* presented *Salafism* first time in Kerala. It is otherwise called as *Salafi* Movement as it invited people to Islam as understood and practiced by the Holy Prophet and the first generation of pious and righteous Muslims *Salafu-Salih*[1]. The stated mission of *Islahi/salafi* movement was to educate believers about superstions and unIslmic practices. It strived hard and made efforts (Jihad) for the propagation of the genuine teachings of Islam (Ahmadkutty 1995: 69-70) and also a progressive outlook in many respects. They modelled a new Islamic theme on the school of thoughts and Islamic renaissance came to pass in Egypt. Around a quarter century, their activism was limited among scholars. Once they realized that reaching out the Muslim grassroots was the only option to spread their words about Salfism. Their purpose remained unaccomplished for a long while. *Kerala Nadvathul Mujahideen* was formed with a mission to pull more crowd into *Salafism*.

KNM dared to declare a departure from unislamic school of thoughts. Monotheism was at the heart of their fundamental *sunnah*[2] and Quranic lessons. The motivated believers to return to monotheism giving up all those different Islamic thoughts prevailed at that time. Their perspectives were comparitively broader. Unlike leaders who shared conservative views, KNM leaders were broad-minded in their approach in presenting Islam. Islam was clearly understood when they introduced Friday *Qutba* in Malayalam. They went further ahead translating the holy *quran* into Malayalam. This helped them influence more faith followers. Moreover, they made a positive impact in the community with their adamant policy against dowry and false traditions which are unfamiliar to true Islam. The reformer organaization was lauded for standing out standing against Islamically unlawful customs. They even opened the gates of masjids for women widely. Crying a fairer gender status for women, they pictured Islam in a different way which Kerala Muslims had not seen before. All those were a few distinct steps in renewing the spirit of Islamic faith among Muslims in Kerala.

Early *Salafi* movement in the state revised the policy Muslims had been following on education. That was considered to be a milestone contribution the organization ever gave to the community. Exposing the limiting sides of *Madrasa* education, Salafi leaders of the time made people aware of the need to refocus on a sythensis of both material and spiritual education. They set up academies all over Kerala. Opened more school gates for girls and led campaigns to popularize education among girls. *Salafis* worked on those reforms and refinements amid an intense rivalry from orthodox clerics and old school organizations. Their hardwork bore fruit albeit facing hardship. The *Islahi* movement also initiated a modern Madrasa system in Kerala to cater to the religious educational needs of boys and girls, and formalized the religious education system. They also established a number of Arabic, Some of them are affiliated to the University of Calicut while others to the University of Kannur. A number of Arts, Science, Technical and private colleges were also established later.

The *SalafÊ* thought is one of the revolutionary movements of Islamic awakening. It was introduced by *salaf* (people of the first three Islamic generations) when the Islamic society faced challenges of misinterpretation from Muslim reverts. The early leaders of the Mujahid movement were able to create revolutionary changes in the social, political, religious, cultural and educational landscapes of Kerala's Muslim community. The *Mujahid* movement represented the progressive trend in the Muslim community in Kerala, challenging orthodoxies as well as the power of the clergy.They promoted modern education among Muslims and encouraged women to learn the letters, and set up schools, colleges and madrasas. They urged Muslims to remain integrated with Kerala's linguistic and cultural heritage. The Islamic philosophy put forth by Jamaludin Afgani, Sheikh Abdu Syed and Rashid Rida moved first-timers of *Mujahid* movement in Kerala (Sullami 2002: 18). Since the first stage of migration to gulf, Salafi philosophy propounded by Ibn Abd al Wahab had inspired Mujahid organization in Kerala. As far as the *Mujahid* movement are concerned this was the beginning of the major shift from the moderate Egyptian *Salafism* to the orthodox Saudi Wahabism.

Ibn-Abd al-Wahab found himself in a situation that was clearly different from the earlier contexts, in a society that, although was politically more stable, was deeply rooted in pagan and innovative (*bidah*) practices. He was convinced that a total acceptance of *Sharia*[3] even in politics was essential for the return to the way of the *Salaf*. He realized that political power was essential for him to propagate the true message of Islam. Afghani led himself into an active role to uplift and revive the spirit and essence of Islam. While Ibn Abd al-Wahab implemented a top-bottom approach[4] of reforming the existing authority and then improving the masses, al-Afghani went in the opposite direction. Fortunately, modern Salfism of Jamaluddin Afghani was more welcome than the Salafism of Abdul Wahab.

At the second half of 1980's, gulf Salafism deepened its influence in Mujahid movement in Kerala. Continued contact with Saudi was the catalyst. Officials in the ministry of religious affairs in Saudi Arabia played a big role in the transformative process. Scholars who went for higher learning sped up the the spread of Salafi ideology. Liberal Salafism of Egypt tradition cleared way for more hard and fast, Islam-to-the-letter Saudi Salafism that was strict to the details of the *Quran*-and-*Hadees*-laid-rules for life. The breed called 'Kerala *Salafis*' were almost extinct and endangered as a result of the invasive idelogolical trend. Also, all these developments paved the way for reforms and progress in the community. The long tradition of Kerala salafism has been white washed with the emergence of Gulf *Salafism* (Gafoor 2016:14). It was the kick off for a renewal of Islamic fashion believers in the state had not seen earlier. Religious go-to-guys were no longer a choice. Go-online popularity for Islamic interpretation picked up. New wave of change hit. It was an on-purpose bid to take Muslims off Sufism and align with global Islam. Additionally, extreme branches of *Salafism* shot off. These consequences had a bearing in defining the religious identity of Muslims in Kerala.

Salafism promoted concept purity of Islam became more popular following migration to gulf regions. More and more youth gravitated to the philosophy *Salafism* presented to them. *Salafism* could powerfully prove that religion was not mere a private spiritual delight but a public exhibition of life portrayed by early role models. The new age *Salafi* pays more careful attention to give a public impression with uncut long beard, above-ankle trouser, moderate body language and more attractive manner of talking. Yemeni Salafism is the most retrogressive form in their tradition. They learn Islam superficially and copy the life of the prophet and followers to the letter.

When Saudi *Whabism/Salafism* was shipped to Kerala in 1990's, frequent splits were in the news. *Yemeni Salafism* or *Dammaj Salafism* came to the fore in the wake of the splits (Vazhakkad 2016: 38). Salafi *School* of Thoughts discussed to-the-letter reading of Islam. Their way was to restore 6th-7th century life. The literal interpretation of *Salafism* advises its followers to flee home to embrace a lifestyle of believers in the old centuries. Since the prophet was a shephered so are they. The prophet lived in the desert, so do they Strangely, from fashion to food, and in everything else, they tread the trail the prophet had left (Vazhakkad 2016: 39). Literal *Salafism* has a detailed way of life instead of the one that is bound by private spiritual journey. Not restricted to ritual devotion and intense divine offerings, *Salfism* goes beyond and creates socio-political impact too. *Dammaj Salafis* who distance from common public to live a reclusive life conveys a message contrary to the secular concepts on which a plural society is deveoped.

After a four decade, *Mujahid* movement seems to be backsliding from the reinvigourating start it had given then. The exodus to gulf dimmed the prospect of Egyptian *Salafi* stream and the predominant Saudi *Salafism* is in place. Focused more on rites and rituals, the renaissance movement has derailed from what it had come into being for. In other words, the movement is inflexible with to-the-letter rites and rituals. Failing to align with the cultural setting of Kerala, *Mujahid* missionary presents textbook Islam. The most dangerous *Salafi* beliefs are those that prohibit the peaceful cohabitation of the believer with those who profess other faiths. Wishing others on non-Islamic festivals, sharing meals with non-believers, etc, are seen as blasphemous acts. The faith system reminds more of the tribal Arabs in the olden days they were full of rites and rituals. It created more demerits than merits.

Jamate Islami's growth and spread, like any other group, too relates to the decades-long movement of life to and fro gulf. Haji V.P Muhammadali., the disciple of Abul Aala Maududi, was the early campaigner and activist of Jamate Islami in Kerala. The first form of *Jamate Islami* Kerala, *Jamatul Murtharshideen* was founded in 1944(Hassan 1998: 138). In 1984, the organization was renamed as *Jamate Islami*. In its primitive stage, its activity and impact limited to an educationally forward micro group (Creamy layer). In 1980's *Jamate Islami* came under the spotlight. It stepped out to connect with common men. One-fourth activists of *Jamate Islami* are working in gulf countries like Qatar, Saudi Arabia, Kuwait, Bahrain, U.A.E and Oman (Hassan 1998:141).

In GCC states, a strong cader group affiliated to *Jamate Islami* is still active working for a common cause. The collective might and organization system of *Jamate Islami* in GCC states is effectively employed for heavy philanthropic works through its different branch groups. Moreover, they routinely execute well-defined training programmes to skill and recruit its activists to top positions in companies and various goverment offices.

Many migrants who were faithful of Sunni philosophy earlier home, make up their mind to work for *Jamate Islami* when they come to gulf. K.A. Siddiq Hassan, former state Ameer of the pan-India organization bears testimony to the fact that there are many migrants who toiled their gulf life to change the whole village home giving time, mind, in kind and in cash(Hassan 1998: 141). Jamate Islami is actively involved socially and culturally through its established network across GCC states. Kerala Islamic Group functioning in Kuwait, Bahrain and Saudi Arabia, Indian Islamic Association in Qatar,

Kerala Islamic association doing service in Muscat, Islamic mission for Indians in Salalah, Islamic Cultural Centre in U.A.E., are the different gulf branch ogranizations to name a few.

Apart from reinforcing its organizational system through various institutions and ventures, Jamate Islami has taken gulf link to create more gains. Jamate Islami is increasingly connecting with mainstream Muslim leaders all over the world. Multiple rewards accrued to it for linking with global maistream Islamic scholars. Jamate Islami, in other words, is networked well with all frontline Islamic associations inside and outside gulf regions. Muslim brotherhood in Egypt, Hamas in Palestine and Annahda in Tunisia are a few leading global Muslim movements to connect. There are also Jamate Islami socio-cultural volunteers in Kerala working for and get paid monthly by global Islamic association Rabitwa. To engage and collaborate with global movements, countries like Qatar is creating common avenues for discourses. This global fraternity of Muslims helped Muslims in Kerala think globally. That's the major rewarding part of the exchanges with global organized movements. Probably, this could be a reason why every single ripple in Muslim world is sent to everyday life of Kerala Muslims also.

Sunnis have comparative gulf influence disavantage in religious affairs and missionary matters when matched with Jamate Islami and Mujahid groups. Both conventional Sunni organizations, the union of scholars Samastha Kerala Jamiyyatul Ulama and samastha faction led by Kanthapuram.A.P. Abubacker Musalyar have the same. Orthodox religious scholars, who are opposed to the renewal process inside and new school of thoughts, themselves kept their groups aloof from global Islamic developments. Soofi way of Sunni tradition in Kerala diverted them from religious rulings and messages pro-ruling-government scholars in gulf states used to give.

Though missionary mechanism, rites and rituals are unifluenced by gulf models, gulf sunni groups copy their organization and modus operandi. All offshoots of the sunni movements are generously receiving finance from gulf countries. However, the sunni groups don't avail of any support from Qatar government which is supporting Jamate Islami and Saudi government that is funding Mujahid groups.

Money is pouring from gulf through these organizations for missionary and religious activism.

A huge share of finance is pouring from NRK's affiliated to various religious organizations. This opportunity has been well handles by A.P. Abubabkar Muslyar led sunni group and Samatha E.K. group doesn't kept their pace. Members are sent to work in variuous gulf states including U.A.E and they are levied a fee. This way, the faction is financing its operations. Kanthapuram group is well-planned and prepared to recruit members to gulf which in turn gurantees a monthly subscription in favour of the group. This fund is reinvested in education and health care with a social cause. Fund need for a range of things like monthly budget of madrasas, masjids, construction of new masjids, charity, education, hospital etc met. In brief, gulf impact is clearly visible like in a broad day light from our way of offering routine prayers to social involvment and political perspective.

Social Relations and Social Structure

Gulf migration and gulf money have brought fundamental changes in the social life of Kerala, especially in the life of Muslim community. Historically, the ownership of land and the caste system were the determinants of Kerala's life. However, the gulf money changed the equilibrium. It transformed the entire visibility of Muslim community in the state. The Malabar Muslim community was shattered economically and politically after the Malabar rebellion 1921. It was the gulf migration that paved new employment opportunities among the community. The gulf migration has helped the migrant households to attain higher level of income, consumption and acquisition of assets, resulting in overall reduction of poverty in Kerala.

It also influenced the socio-political life of the community. It revamped the social stratification relations among the community. Malabar Muslim community took a new step forward in the socio-political life of Kerala. The villages, which are taken as the case studies for the thesis, are Muslim dominated villages. Traditionally, agriculture is the main income source for the people. Even the non-Muslims communities were also found agriculture as their main income source. There were land owners among the Muslims, however, the participation in government jobs were merely none. Apart from agriculture and agriculture related jobs, trading was the next income source among the community. There were few aristocratic families among the community, who enjoyed special privilege in public and religious circles.

On 1980s it has started to change. A new economic force has emerged through the gulf migration. Up to the second half of the 1970s the above mentioned aristocratic families and the very few government employees were the elite in the society. The lower social strata of the society have been dependent of the elite. The migration and the gulf money ended this dependence.

In 1970s, the remaining social order has started to shake. A large number of economically backward Muslims emerged as a new economic force after the migration to the gulf. They are started to getting a new priority in the society. They also started to participate heavily on the new social formation. Gulf migrants cannot settle away but must, sooner or later return home where their new found wealth and access to consumption may dramatically alter their status and their relationships with others, and offer them the chance to forge new identities (Osella 2000: 119).

The newly emerged economic class gradually reached high rank on social standing. The influence of migration experience on widening of the horizons of interest and broadening of perspectives has also been significant and positive (Nair 1986: 06). Along the financial betterment, the gulf migration also helped to the migrant labors to attain more international life experience and exposure. This also contributed to attaining higher acceptance in the social standing of the society. "Gulf money has played a major role in restructuring the Kerala society, at a rate never before experienced in the state. From the bottom five percent of the income ladder, some of the Gulf Non-Resident Keralites(NRKs) have gone up all the way to the top five percent, transcending family background, caste or creed.(Zakariah 2004: 50).

This transition transformed the social structure in a large extend. The NRKs were started to get appointed in the organizational and authoritative positions of the community institutions and organizations.

Their opinions and decisions were also considered in a prime importance. It changed the social relations. Apart from the aristocratic families, government employees, traders, farmers, and agricultural labors, a new category called, *Gulfkar* (gulf migrants), made appearance in the society. "Money brought power with it. The lure for power developed. It was a necessary result of the migration (Suresh 2006). Technological advancements have further strengthened the migrants'links with the home countries on a day-to-day basis. The migrants make efforts to sustain their relations with the sending country through transnational religious practices as well (Levitt, Peggy.(2004) In this way, Gulf migration has been instrumental in democratization of Muslim society in Kerala. It's no surprise to see that migration to gulf destinations send a wind of democratic change in Muslim community.

Although Muslim social hierarchy cannot be termed as 'feudal' in the fullest sense, it was semi-feudal to some extent. Traditionally land-owned rich ancestral families always ruled the roost as they were at the helm of Muslim society. They had a commanding voice over religious institutions and every day business of the society. The quick economic progress in the wake of migration to gulf revolutionized the people at the bottom of the society. Priorities changed so did the participation of the poor as economic boom following gulf migration helped the voiceless to be heard. They were even received by those traditionally dominant families. The poor class were earlier unwelcome to those families. Gradually, the unwelcome class climbed to the equal level of opinion making mainstream. The wealthy Muslims, who had been controlling the whole affairs of the institutions and organizations affiliated to Muslim community, were replaced by the emerging upstarts from the base.

Family Structure and Status of Women

Taken all the parameters of women's empowerment in State, Gulf migration and the consequent changes contributed much in restructuring the internal structure of the family and accelerating women's progress towards a new society. The family structure of the Mappila Muslims were patrilineal, patrilocal and strongly patriarchal.

Women and children were received any importance in the decision making process of the families. The decisions among the families always took by either fathers or husbands. In public and in familiar ceremonies, fathers or husbands were the sole representives of single families.

However, when almost all adults in a family sailed to gulf regions as migrant labors, a vacuum of male representatives of families has emerged. It gave new opportunities for the women in the families. They started to come forward, handing the day-today activities of the families. Taking care of children's education, attending family functions, constituting ceremonial functions etc are now became the responsibilities of the women in the families. Grand mothers, mothers and elder sisters were became main decision makers in the families. Along with the new sort of decision makers, the elder boys in the families also received prime importance in familiar decision makings. The subtle transformation that has taken place among the Gulf wives would have a more lasting imprint on the Kerala society than any material changes which migration has brought about (Zakariah 2000: 45). It accelerated the democratisation process among the Muslim families in the state.

Gulf migration has helped bring about a remarkable change in the social hierarchy and women empowerment. Rather than the women empowerment drive in the community, the shift in social scenario is mainly caused by gulf migration. It cuts two ways as to how gulf migration is a catalyst to women empowerment. The financial jump in as a result of gulf migration made an incredible advancement in education. Where the state failed to fare well, the community focused well to provide better education. Moreover, money produced in the oil-rich migration destination of liquid gold, paved the way for Muslim community taking the advantage of self-financing education.

In the early 1990s, backward Malabar in terms of the proportion of educational facilities witnessed commencing of countless educational institutions. In that way, expatriate society helped government to surmount the regional imbalance in the allocation of educational resources. The new educational trend set following the exponential growth of academic institutions provided more avenues for girls to experience experiment and explore a wealth of knowledge and excel in academic performance. Consequently, more and more girls enrolled in for new breed of courses offered. Muslim society had always turned away from boarding education for girls. As newly set up educational institutions reduced the distance from home, there was a huge influx of willing students. Interestingly, with more avenues for professional education, the more amount of spending on education became the order of the day. Well-educated girls had bigger role and great recognition in the society. They were heard and had their space in the family and society alike.

All these dramatic developments changed the scenario in favour of women. In the male-dominated society, women found more space for opinion. In the organized work places, more and more Muslim women joined which was again a natural consequence of the lift in education. Women became the main bread winner in many families. Windfall remittances at the disposal and the absence of husbands have its impact on the work participation of women in Kerala. A study on migration shows not only that wives of emigrant husbands were on average better educated but a significantly higher proportion of them (84%) reported being housewives than the proportion of all women (60.9%). This financial freedom of women made their voice heard. Another significant aspect was the developments in the marriage market. Marriages, once believed to be the domain of male-opinion, got transformed into an equal chance of choice and opinion for both male and female. Through advancement in education, marriages turned out to be a social agreement to safeguard the interest of both bride and groom.

Women marched to progressive roles in the society. Their freedom of expression and financial self-sufficiency empowered them. Besides, gulf families allocated more resources for girls for education and marriage. Changing habit of the spending remittances is the major qualitative change in the attitude of the Gulf migrants. In the beginning of the second decade of Gulf migration, they shifted their focus of spending on the construction on big houses and shopping complex to provide better education to their children. Now providing better education to their children is the first priority of a migrant. Another important social consequence of the remittances was their effect on the power structure of the household and community. The remittances were almost always sent to the account of the wives .Thus; younger women were even more included in the family affairs than their husbands had been living with them. The social status of the women who are handling the remittances independently, automatically increased. "A healthy wind of social change is blowing across the entire rural areas of Kerala, thanks to a considerable extent, to the impact that the migration phenomenon has had on women's status in society in this state (Nair and Pillai 1994: 25).

Nuclear families needed more shelters. Multiplying homes sped up the destruction of joint family system. Nuclear families empowered women like never before. Bread winners, in most cases are husbands, go abroad. More responsibilities are on wives once husbands make their way to earn a living abroad. A range of responsibilities from managing household to taking care of the everyday education of children were on the wives of expatriates. They attended P.T.A meeting, went to bank for transactions and local administrative offices for clearing papers, and did even shopping filling the gap of their husbands abroad. Thus, representing themselves and home head abroad, the grass widows started doing commendable job. This paved the way for much public space for women.

Social gatherings like marriages; parties etc. are one of the venues of socialization. Since males are abroad, women have began to attend these functions which increased the opportunities for establishing new relationships and thereby the means more socialization. The newly attained socializations and the decision making powers of the wives of gulf migrants instinctively brought them to the heads of the families and it extensively contributed to the confidant building of these women. They became more aware, confident and energetic. "With the passage of years, as wives learn to manage things on their own, they tend more and more to take independent decision on many matters and in the process want to be less and less dependent on relatives. They also gain in confidence so as to live independently Gulati 1987:42). The foreign experience and exposure to diverse cultures and civilizations has broadened the vision of the migrants in respect of the sharing of household duties and responsibilities and financial management with spouses and other members of the household (Nair 1986: 64).

The exposure made them to respect independent individuality of women, especially their wives' individuality. Through the successful family management and utilization of the new decision making powers, the wives of migrant labour matured into more confident and independent women. it is actually a revolution in a highly patriarchal Kerala society. The independent life made them more self-reliant and confident. So the Gulf migration, no doubt, did more than any other factor including the works of reformative organisations in the transformation of women, especially Muslim women in Malabar.The frequent interaction with the social institututions and the active participation in social gathering has also broadened the social outlook as well as the political understanding of the Gulf wives in a tremendous way.

The three selected villages for this study showed housewives getting more sensitive and sensible about the pulse of local, national and global politics. There is a detailed reference in the studies carried out by Leela Gulati and Philappo Osallo. These kinds of engagements have empowered their social interaction and mobility.The migration also helped the very common people to showing keen interest in international news and developments. The instinct is to know about countries and places where their beloved are working, especially husbands, sons, fathers, brothers and other relatives. It changed the global outlook of the Muslim women. "As a result, the general awareness of developments around the world is considerably better in the migrant households as compared to non-migrant households (Gulati 1993:113). Kerala's higher media literacy is a direct outcome of these aspirations. It also enriched the Muslim media houses throughout the state.

Even though the gulf migration positively engaged in Muslim modernization especially in empowering of women and the democratization of family structure, it also drawn scars in the life of the migrant labours and their families. In situations where an individual moves and the rest of the family remains, there is a host of possible consequences for the remaining family or houschold unit which are often ignored (Oberoi 1987: 57). Almost 93 percent of gulf migrants are men. Among them 80 percentage of people are under the age of 44 to 25. Some other study shows 67.16 percent of migrant labours are under the age 30 years. The impact of migration upon the family members to the emigrants, who are left behind, is immense. Gulf wives are a term used to describe married women in Kerala households whose husbands work/live in Gulf countries. Kerala Migration Survey 2011 conducted by the Centre for Development Studies shows that emigration to the Gulf region from Kerala stood at 2.28 million in 2011 and there were an estimated 1.1 million Gulf Wives in the state, running the family and bringing up the children with or without the help of their extended family.

It is very obvious that male migration widens women's agency in decision making and managing the family and finances in the absence of a paterfamilias/male head of a family and thereby empower them substantially. However, the wives stay behind and spend long years separated from their husbands working in Gulf countries have impacted on them socially and psychologically in extensively. The social pressure upon the Gulf wives, the loneliness they suffer, effects of adolescent child birth, pressure of child rearing, sexual moroseness and the resultant psychological trauma, gulf wives had suffer a lot. Despite whatever economic/social empowerment they have attained, they had pay a huge price for that.

The growth of Muslim Press

In the early years of 19th century, Kerala Mulsims had entered media field. Even before that, there were a few magazines in Arabic-Malayalam script, which weren't big hits. Following the formation of Muslim Aikya Sangham, the Muslim press units grew up discussing more community news. 'Chandrika' was the first ever daily published by Muslim Printing and Publishing Company which was set up in 1936. After a half century, 'Madhyamam' was launched. The gulf finance and fans made 'Madhyamam' a tangible dream. Today there are six dailies different Muslim groups are publishing from the state. Among the print media, 'Madhyamam' is a mainstream daily with dedicated decades to its credit. Even before independence, many Muslim movements had ventured into journalism. However, none of them lasted. All other news papers other than 'Chandrika', was launched after the second half of the decade during which gulf migration gained momentum. A great share of lifeblood-finance for starting and sustaining the dailies came from gulf always. Most of the dailies are still alive thanks to the gulf funding. Because of the press presence, there is a visible makeover in the way Muslims are today. The media representing Muslims have effectively shaped the cultural and political views of people with the news covered round-the-clock.

There are magazines under the Muslim managements which are dealing national and international politics to health, children and family topics. Almost all of Muslim organizations are releasing category based magazines. However, the Muslim magazines are directly dependent to gulf migration. The income sources of the most magazines are from gulf countries. Majority of subscription and advertisement revenues are from gulf countries. Madhymam, chandrika, tejas, Siraj, Vathamanam and Suprabhatham the main dailies published by Muslim organisations. Except Chandrika, all of other five dailies are only started after the second decade of gulf migration. Chandrika, started on 1938 from Thalassery, is only daily which having a pre migration history.

The all dailies are managed by six different Muslim organizations. It is a commendable achievement for a community, which was most backward community in terms of education historically. Even the most forward community of the state, Nair community and the ezhava community, majority community in the state, were not able to handle their own dailies in the state. Deepika daily is the only daily run by a Christian community organisation. The great success in the publication is the direct evidence of gulf migration and its positive impact on socio-political awareness of the community. The publications are intensively helped to the democratisation process of Kerala Muslim community and it also helped the community in gaining unimaginable socio-political advantage. The publications are successfully built an independent social narrative for the community and made a brilliant engagement with mainstream media houses in the state.

Media also contributed to the strengthening of exclusiveness of the Muslims in Malabar. The large scale production of literary works grounded in Islam provided them a separate identity. The media undermined the authority of rural Ulemas who were the sole custodian of Islamic knowledge and its transmission through Dars and religious sermons. Democratisation of theology was disliked by the traditional ulemas. Gulf migration also helped the Muslims to achieve horizontal solidarity within the community which subsequently helped to achieve a measure of social cohesion in a diversified and even culturally polarized community. Again the idea of an Islamic unity, based on equality of believers, began to gain ground disappear the social iniqualities among the Muslims in Malabar.

Notes

1. Those who lived during the life time of the Prophet and happened to learn Islamicpractices from the original source.
2. *Sunnah* the verbally transmitted record of the teachings, deeds and sayings, silent permissions (or disapprovals) of the Islamic prophet Muhammad, as well as various reports about Muhammad's companions.
3. Islamic canonical law based on the teachings of the Koran and the traditions of the Prophet (Hadith and Sunna).
4. One of the reformational theory starts from the rulers and leaders in order to reform the followers.

Chapter - 7

Finding the Shore

Kerala witnessed deep-rooted change in the social hierarchy during 1970s. Land reforms and gulf migration helped the state society progress in a big way. The beneficiary peasants of land reforms and expatriates earned a living abroad became the major force of social change and the strength of economy during this decade. Following land reform, the well-to-do landlords who owned large share of land had to give up the lion share of it and poor peasants received free land. Consequently, this shook the landlord-tenant relationship and social life those days. When a big part of the populace lived at the bottom stair of the social status ladder received title to free land, there was a huge social uplift.

However, it was the gulf migration that changed the destiny of Muslims society. Started since 1970s, gulf migration has had an unparalleled transformation in the socio-economic life in Kerala. The lifestyle change after gulf migration is evidently present across a wide spectrum of people especially Muslims in Kerala. Aside from redefining the economic life of Muslim community, the frequent gulf flights to gulf helped the change their socio-political outlook. The influence is found not only in private life of individuals (micro level) but also in the family (meso level) and public life (macro level).

Influence on individuals

Gulf migration has changed the way individuals are socially involved. Men at grassroots were adventurously ready to embark to find pot of gold at the end of the rainbow. The other side was always greener as unemployment was extreme and poverty severe. Against all odds, they kept sailing to find a career abroad. That being the case, those who voyaged with rising risk belonged to the class whose main issue was their bread and butter. Oil-money helped the construction sector in gulf nations climb and that resulted in huge demand for manpower. The surge in construction projects turned out to be big blessings for unskilled labours from the state. Not only a plethora of new jobs came up but also better pay packets the employees were able to wait for. In the second half of 1970s and '80s, an average worker in gulf sector had received higher pay than a government employee in the state. Those common people who found it hard to earn a living home were the pioneers of gulf migration and it awakened the whole population in social and economic terms. The wind of change lifted individuals, their families and societies too they belonged to.

The large scale migration to the Middle East of lower class migrants and their rapid enrichment brought about a reconstruction of the ethnic identities of Muslims in Kerala. A new breed of economically self-reliant well-off class rose from the backward section at the bottom of the social hierarchy like Ossan and Poolsan. Muslim social hierarchy got restructured as a result. Life took new direction as wealth accumulated so does their social status. Majority of them assumed more social responsibilities their own way. Expatriates literally still maintained service-to-society mindset despite the fair fact that the traditionally wealthy landlords and government employees were all self-reliant through secure sources of revenue. The higher they made it to the top of social hierarchy, the more they were socially committed.

The expatriates helped their relatives in the first place. After that, they helped their friends and neighbors out. With big hearts, they cleared visa procedures to recruit close relatives and friends to gulf. In the early times, there was almost an unconditional service motive in getting visa issued for the gulf-aspiring family members and folks back home. However, the scenario changed in the mid 1980s. Visa was no longer a free offer but sale for an agreed price. Expatriates were bread winners of their family and helping hand to their folks at the same time. Thus the social network got proliferated. Democratizing societies, the socially and economically surged section busted the long-going social hierarchy.

It was very clear that a poor person had only to write to a Gulf migrant from his area if he had any major or unexpected expenses to meet.The friends in need gulf expatriates were friends indeed. It was quite usual to post letters narrating the sorry story home in hard times. Expatriates always swung into action sending home even loaned money abroad. It was a matter of honor for the migrants to respond to such a request. In addition, there were local committees for each gulf pocket, usually organized by the local mosque to take care of the poor. The local community also felt a sense of responsibility for widows and orphans without any relatives to help them.

There were four main ways in which help was rendered in the initial days of the migration. Money was given to help poor families build a "pucca" (concrete) house; to provide a dowry to get a girl married; and to support the local orphanage. Finally, migrant households provided food to poor families and clothes when the migrant returned from the Gulf. Mushrooming multiple local charitable movements sustained because of generous financing by hardworking expatriates. Their service ranges from raising roof for the homeless, medical treatment for poor patients, free food items for the starving section, wedding arrangement for unfortunate girls of marriageable age etc. the long list of humanitarian help entitles expatriates the big credit.

More philanthropists and Samaritans emerged as the family heads extended their role and reach beyond their call of household duty to serve society in a big way. Honours are due to expatriates with such Samaritan roles they took helping society.With generous supply of donated money from gulf, it's quite clear that Muslim community institutions and organizations in Kerala have comparative advantage over their counterparts in other states. The charity organisations are being used as a strategic platform to transform the economic capital earned from migration to achieve social prestige, status and legitimacy in the home society. In other words, these spaces are being utilized by the migrants to display the newly acquired socio-economic mobility and also to demolish the feudatory class structure in Muslim community.

Changes in the power structure within the community

Gulf migration has been instrumental in democratization of Muslim society in Kerala. It's no surprise to see that migration to gulf destinations send a wind of democratic change in Muslim community. The apparent signs of democratic development are still there in the society and the basic institutions called families. Although Muslim social hierarchy cannot be termed as 'feudal' in the fullest sense, it was semi-feudal to some extent. Traditionally land-owned rich ancestral families always ruled the roost as they were at the helm of Muslim society. They had a commanding voice over religious institutions and every day business of the society. Quite often, those ruling families and scholars had the final word on religious matters. Those who rose to high ranks were the literate land-owned wealthy class. The creamy class always came up the top of social pyramid. They were a standalone class in the society. Even though Islam is free from caste-discrimination, economic inequality was dominant like a system of caste curse. In fact, people at the base of social pyramid had to remain slaves of the filthy rich ancestral families.

The quick economic progress in the wake of migration to gulf revolutionized the people at the bottom of the society. Priorities changed so did the participation of the poor as economic boom following gulf migration helped the voiceless to be heard. They were even received by those traditionally dominant families. The poor class were earlier unwelcome to those families. Gradually, the unwelcome class climbed to the equal level of opinion making mainstream. The wealthy Muslims, who had been controlling the whole affairs of the institutions and organizations affiliated to Muslim community, were replaced by the emerging upstarts from the base. The big beneficiaries of the impacting shift after gulf migration were the marginalized section in the community. With the transformation in social conditions, the form of patronage given to religion has also undergone change. Earlier, Hadramaut Sayyids emigrated from Yemen to become spiritual leaders in the region. But it is now easy for ideas and messages to emigrate, without the physical presence of the emigrants.

Changing status of women

The family structure of the Mappila Muslims were patrilineal, patrilocal and strongly patriarchal. Though the seclusion of women and their early marriage were ideals. Gulf migration has helped bring about a remarkable change in the social hierarchy and women empowerment. Rather than the women empowerment drive in the community, the shift in social scenario is mainly caused by gulf migration. It cuts two ways as to how gulf migration is a catalyst to women empowerment. The financial jump in as a result of gulf migration made an incredible advancement in education. Where the state failed to fare well, the community focused well to provide better education. Moreover, money produced in the oil-rich migration destination of liquid gold, paved the way for Muslim community taking the advantage of self-financing education.

In the early 1990s, backward Malabar in terms of the proportion of educational facilities witnessed commencing of countless educational institutions. In that way, expatriate society helped government to surmount the regional imbalance in the allocation of educational resources. The new educational trend set following the exponential growth of academic institutions provided more avenues for girls to experience experiment and explore a wealth of knowledge and excel in academic performance. Consequently, more and more girls enrolled in for new breed of coursed offered. Muslim society had always turned away from boarding education for girls. As newly set up educational institutions reduced the distance from home, there was a huge influx of willing students. Interestingly, with more avenues for professional education, the more amount of spending on education became the order of the day. Well-educated girls had bigger role and great recognition in the society. They were heard and had their space in the family and society alike.

All these dramatic developments changed the scenario in favour of women. In the male-dominated society, women found more space for opinion. In the organized work places, more and more Muslim women joined which was again a natural consequence of the lift in education. Women became the main bread winner in many families. This financial freedom of women made their voice heard. Another significant aspect was the developments in the marriage market. Marriages, once believed to be the domain of male-opinion, got transformed into an equal chance of choice and opinion for both male and female. Through advancement in education, marriages turned out to be a social agreement to safeguard the interest of both bride and groom.

Empowered women were able to challenge and change the cursed social evil called dowry. They shattered the bargain system by means of progress in education. As dowry was an outdated thing in the marriage market, the priorities of gulf money spending got reset. Owning a concrete home had always topped the wish-list and the surplus was earmarked for marrying away daughter(s). However, when education became the first choice over anything else, more investment went to help offspring earn higher degrees. Women empowerment was never the planned purpose to be achieved. It was not by choice but by chance the improvement in women education came to pass. Somehow, all those transformation boiled down to the strengthening of women as a whole.

Women marched to progressive roles in the society. Their freedom of expression and financial self-sufficiency empowered them. Besides, gulf families allocated more resources for girls for education and marriage. Another important social consequence of the remittances was their effect on the power structure of the household and community. The remittances were almost always sent to the account of the wives .Thus; younger women were even more included in the family affairs than their husbands had been living with them. Changing habit of the spending remittances is the major qualitative change in the attitude of the Gulf migrants. In the beginning of the second decade of Gulf migration, they shifted their focus of spending on the construction on big houses and shopping complex to provide better education to their children. Now providing better education to their children is the first priority of a migrant.

Nuclear families needed more shelters. Multiplying homes sped up the destruction of joint family system. Nuclear families empowered women like never before. Bread winners, in most cases are husbands, go abroad. More responsibilities are on wives once husbands make their way to earn a living abroad. A range of responsibilities from managing household to taking care of the everyday education of children were on the wives of expatriates. They attended P.T.A meeting, went to bank for transactions and local administrative offices for clearing papers, and did even shopping filling the gap of their husbands abroad. Thus, representing themselves and home head abroad, the grass widows started doing commendable job. This paved the way for much public space for women. Such a public interaction creates clearer socio-political perspectives among women. The three select villages for this study showed housewives getting more sensitive and sensible about the pulse of local, national and global politics. There is a detailed reference in the studies carried out by Leela Gulati and Philappo Osallo. This kinds of engagements have empowered their social interaction and mobility.

Press and the presence of gulf resources

Nationally, Kerala is the exception proves the rule when it comes to Muslims create and control press. There are six dailies different Muslim groups are publishing from the state. Among the print media, 'Madhyamam' is a mainstream daily with dedicated decades to its credit. Even before independence, many Muslim movements had ventured into journalism. However, none of them lasted. All other news papers other than 'Chandrika', was launched after the second half of the decade during which gulf migration gained momentum. A great share of lifeblood-finance for starting and sustaining the dailies came from gulf always. Most of the dailies are still alive thanks to the gulf funding. Because of the press presence, there is a visible makeover in the way Muslims are today. The media representing Muslims have effectively shaped the cultural and political views of people with the news covered round-the-clock.

Social Scientists have frequently noted the importance of media in furthering community formation. Following Benedict Anderson's assertion about nations being imagined communities and identities. The pan Islamic sentiment also had given a additional fillip to the emergence of separate Muslim identity. The Muslim media also played a major role in strengthening the Muslim identity in Malabar.

Indisputably, gulf migration has transformed the cultural life of Muslims in Kerala in a big way. Muslim community as a recognized identity, engage in exchanges with the general public and get involved in cultural and political activities as well. Cultural exchanges of the sort enabled Muslims in Kerala to be more socially included unlike their counterparts in others states in the country. In this way media contributed to the strengthening of inclusiveness and visibility of the Muslims in Malabar in the socio-political domain in Kerala.

In the early years of 19th century, Mulsims had entered media field. Even before that, there was a few magazines in Arabic-Malayalam script, which weren't big hits. Following the formation of Muslim Aikya Sangham, the Muslim press units grew up discussing more community news. 'Chandrika' was the first ever daily published by Musqlim Printing and Publishing Company which was set up in 1936. After a half century, 'Madhyamam' was launched. The gulf finance and fans made 'Madhyamam' a tangible dream.

Media also contributed to the strengthening of exclusiveness of the Muslims in Malabar. The large scale production of literary works grounded in Islam provided them a separate identity. The media undermined the authority of rural Ulemas who were the sole custodian of Islamic knowledge and its transmission through Dars and religious sermons. Democratisation of theology was disliked by the traditional ulemas. Gulf migration also helped the Muslims to achieve horizontal solidarity within the community which subsequently helped to achieve a measure of social cohesion in a diversified and even culturally polarized community.

Community-institutions-building

Migrants have played an assertive role in community-institution-building in Kerala Muslim society. They have also set up thousands of institutions that cater to the community-not just Madrasas and Mosques, as in much of north India, but also schools, colleges, hospitals, orphanages, industrial centres, banks, newspapers and so on. These institutions have been based on remittances from outside, and all rival factions among the Muslim organizations have mobilized money from the gulf. The Islamic principle of zakat has been quite effectively used in this mobilization as contributions for such pious activities become a religious duty.

Madrassas

Gulf migration has played pivotal role in making Madrassa system in Kerala more detailed and scientific. Madrassa system is well-managed across Kerala while the situation doesn't prevail in other states. The institutions offer a comprehensive and scientific education on religion. Samastha Kerala Islam Matha Vidhyabhyasa Board, Kerala Sunni Vidhyabhyasa Board, Mujahid, Jamate Islami- there are four education boards for Madrassas under the major Muslim organizations. Over fifteen lakhs students are attending from grade one to higher Madrassa classes in Kerala. (Anees Vaavad, Matha Padanathinte Kerala Model-Sathya Saraniyude Charithra Saakshyam 2012-842-44). One lakh fifty thousand new students arrive Madrassa every year. One lakh twenty five thousand teachers work in Madrassas across Kerala. Unique part of Madrassas in Kerala is the buildings and books and the organization of the system compared to Madrassas outside Kerala.

In north India most students in Madrasas come from poor families, many of who join Madrasas simply because they cannot afford to go to regular schools. In contrast, most students in Kerala come out of choice and interest in becoming religious scholars from quite well-off families and not out of economic compulsion. Because most of the Madrassas and the Arabic colleges in state teach both Islamic and modern subjects, parents from middle-class families are enthusiastic to send their children to these institutions. In other parts of India, on the other hand, because few Madrasas have proper arrangements for teaching modern subjects, middle-class parents hesitate to send their children there to study. Teachers are well versed in moral and material lessons taught at these Madrassas. Madrassa teachers too earn a decent living because of gulf migration.

Better salary and situations at work made Madrassa more than a moral education. And more teachers joined the field to grab increasingly attractive jobs. Till the last years of the second decade of the Gulf migration, a Musliyar,(the teachers of the local Madrassa is called also he is assigned with the duty of leading the compulsory prayers in the mosque) was literally the most exploited one in the labor sector and is expected to be involved in daily religious services, in exchange of a meager wage. Today the whole situation has been changed and the Madrassa teaching has became a better part time job in the sense of finance as well as prestige. According to the latest statistics more than twenty five lakhs madrassa teachers has been working under various Madrassa boards in the State.

Though the Madrassa system has been systematic and scientific in its administration, infrastructure and curriculam, there was no fecilities for higher studies above higher secondary level. To address this issue various Muslim organisations started a number of Colleges to provide religious education along with the general education. The main motive of these institutions to prepare scholars who have a good understanding of both Islam and modern society so that they can serve community better and more effectively. The leading organisation had a clear-cut idea that the Ulema need knowledge of modern subjects in addition to Islamic subjects. After all, they have to provide guidance to the community not just in ritual matters but in all other spheres of personal and collective life.

Gulf money also contributed by increasing the number and range of people who were involved in exchange and dependency relationships and by creating new religious institutions in the community. Their identity as fellow Mappila Muslims was constantly used to stress the necessity for charity, brotherhood and equality. A good deal of money also went to the support of the local mosques and to the schools and colleges imparting religious training. These kinds of solidarity due to the charity and support mechanaism by the Gulf migrants made the effort of the community leaders to organize the muslim mass under their banner. In short the identity assertion followed by the gulf support is one of the main reason to organize the community.

Major changes occurred in the form and functioning of the religious denominations

Noticeable lifestyle change has come to pass due to continuous contact with Arab world. The influence is not only in the ideology and modus operandi of the religious organizations but also found in the performing of everyday prayers and rituals. Here, this study is all about how gulf link moved the mainstream Muslim movements like Sunnis, Salafis and Jamate Islami. The collective conclusion of this study points to the fact that Salfization is the major change in the direction Kerala Muslim society travelled since the early days of migration.

In another means the Gulf relation has been an instrumental for the transformation of popular Islam in to the slow and steady emergence of Scriptual Islam. The successors of sufi ancestry took a new religious road as gulf migration caused ideological influence. Regular exchanges between a section of gulf expatriates and salafi clerics in Saudi Arabia pressed Muslims in kerala to give up Egyptian Salafi lineage and embrace Gulf Salfi style. The tectonic shift from Egyptian Salafi spiritual stream, which always considered the socio-political background of the audience society, into the word-by-word discipline in Islamic lessons the gulf Salafism practised unfolded a new Muslim thought-stream, lifestyle and cultural tradition.

Salafisation of Kerala Muslims

Till the second half of twentieth century, Muslims in Kerala was not well organized. The prophet's devoted descendants called Sayyids sailed across Arabian sea from Hadr Mawth to make it to yet unknown Kerala. Muslim society registered progressive development receiving messages from the descendants and the well read researchers in the holy Quran. Along with the two kinds of leadership mentioned here, there was another kind of leadership who took the advantage their ancestral family status to occupy the position. Notwithstanding all those advantages at hand, Muslims were still uncoordinated at large. Moreover, their presence was only felt within the limited local geography.

Malabar riots helped trigger serious talks about organizing Muslims as a consolidated unit. A broad sense of unity called Pan Kerala Muslim Identity figured in the discussions. Such a serious deliberation, discussion and discourse ended up in the formation of Muslim Aikya Sangham at Kodungallur in 1924. Muslim Aikya Sangham and Kerala Jam Iyyathul Ulama were the first concerted

Muslim movements in Kerala. These organizations were influenced by Egyptian salafi philosophy. In a nutshell, the story of Muslim organized movement in Kerala is a part of the history of Egyptian salafism.

The early leadership of Jamiyyathul Ulama and its offshoot Mujahid movement followed and spread the word the school of thought put forth by Muslim world intellectuals like Rashid Ridha, Muhammad Abdu and Jamaludin Afgani. Saudi Salafism gradually crowded out Egyptian Salafism as a result of gulf migration. Even the followers of pure Sufi tradition were not exempted from the Salafi influence. However, Saudi Salafism in Sunni section was not so deep-seated and strong as in Mujahid movements. There was a revision in the way Jamate Islami worked too thanks to the gulf migration. Jamathe Islami depends more on Qatar for its source of finance.

Mujahid movement- the road from *Egyptian Salafism* to *Saudi Salafism*

The renaissance Mujahid movement came up with a fresh hope to renew Muslim society. At first they came to be known as Islahi movement. Later, they progressed receiving the new title 'Salafis' led by a flock of revivalist leaders. The ideological background of the Islahi movement in Kerala was the revivalist thought of the Egyptian Salafi scholars lead by the scholars such as Jamal din Afghani, Muhammed Abdu and Rashid Rida. Their thoughts moved and motivated early-time Salafi scholars.

The Islahi leaders were not at all influenced by the Gulf Salafism which was initiated by Muĺammed ibn Abd al-Wahhab in Najd which is located in today's Saudi Arabia in the initial years of the Muslim renaissance movement in the state. These tradition has been transformed by the first half of the 1980s when the Gulf migration reaches its peak. It was in this period the Mujahid movement came under the influence of Saudi brand of Salafism which is the orthodox and inaward looking form of Salafi tradition in the World.

In the second decade of the migration to gulf, skilled labours were the catalyst of the transition. The category of working class had cushy jobs and better work environment. Many Malayali expatriates had an inside track in the affairs of the ruling machinery in the region. This favourable situation led to creating collaboration between religious leadership in Kerala and the state office for religious matters in countries like Saudi Arabia. The opportunity to engage with the offices was indeed a stroke of blessings to the religious organizations in Kerala. Continuous contact with the religious affairs office in those countries built a bridge of friendship. Most mainstream movements took advantages of this harmony and received generous help from the countries. The fund thus flowed helped them build up their organizational strength in Kerala.

This is happening olny because of the influence of constant relation between the leaders of Salafi movement in Kearala and saudi regime. As I mentioned earlier this was happening in the first half of the 1980s that is the stable stage of the gulf migration from the state. A number of Salafi preachers and leaders went to Saudi Arabia for higher studies in Islamic Fiqh and jurisprudence. They tried to copied the customes and patterns of Saudi religious leaders in to the religious life of the Muslims in Kerala. These kinds of changes in preach and practices of the religion is very evident in the social life of Muslims in the state. With the gulf boom, the reformist movements came to be reliant upon Wahabism and Salafism more in terms of funding and organizing power, than on their earlier ideological dependency.

Rise of *Neo Salafism* in Kerala Context

Since gulf Salafism spread across the length and breadth of the state, there has been a pointed attempt to relocate the religion from the living premises to closed-room spiritual routines. The phenomenon widely known as Neo Salafism sent shockwaves across the sphere of plural culture prevalent in the state. Focused fully on religious rituals, Neo Salafism featured a kind of spiritual extremism. Cut off the engaging communication with the plural society, the move Of exclusion endangered social diversity. The extremist expression of spiritual ecstasy added fuel to the fire of the self imposed exclusion. Changed attitude, new attire, breakaway from socio-cultural involvement and lifestyle difference detached a section of Muslims from the general society.

Widely trending modified manner of clothing, veiling face, wearing hand gloves and socks etc can be attributed to the message Mujahid movement disseminated. In brief, Islahi movement later turned out to be the most regressive form. They mistook the fashion of aged Arab tribes for the actual faith of Islam. To sum up, it was Mujahid Group which illustrates how a 'Kerala Muslim' got transformed into a 'Malayali Muslim'. At the later period the same movement began to teach how a Malayali Muslim transformed in to a Global. Arab Muslim. In this way the organisation transformed itself. The Gulf relation has been an instrumental for the transformation of popular Islam in to the slow and steady emergence of Scriptural Islam.

Jamaathe Islami Hind

With comparatively less number of memberships to its credit and claim, Jamate Islami is one of the frontline Muslim organizations in Kerala. The organization doesn't represent even one-sixth of the members lining up under the banner of EK Sunni group. However, Jamate Islami plays a significant role as a trend setter in the community. Gulf money is the reason for this achievement. They own and manage majority of Muslim media in Kerala. But undoubtedly, it is Jamaath that kept abreast of the time and made themselves visible in the printing and educational sectors, courtesy to their corporate exploration of opportunities carefully utilizing the gulf money.

Perhaps, Jamate Islami can do itself proud of the well planned productivity it creates out of the gulf money. Apart from educating their members in religious matters, Jamate Islami focuses well on orienting members to the contemporary socio-political developments across the globe. Mahallus where Jamat workers outnumber the rest of the groups, Jama'at members share a definitive and better political position than others. Jamaate Islami is streets ahead in many areas especially in providing political literacy to women. Even the housewives are well informed and concerned about the common Muslim grievances within and the outside the country. It's the white collar working professionals who are the strong financial source of Jama'ate Islami whereas th0usands of blue collar workers at the base of the social pyramid sustain the Sunni sections of the society. Jama'ate

Islami, the middleclass movement has been able to reach out to the members at the grassroots.

Sunni Factions

There is no scientific statistics about the population of each religious group. Given the account of each group running institutions in Mahallus, Sunni groups can be said to be dominating. Samastha EK group is more dominant than others. EK group by default, unless he/ she personally moved out of the circle deliberately buying into a different ideology of a competing faction. Following a very flexible organizational set-up, this group exists in villages under the dominion of some traditional feudal families. Sunni sections never compromise on their conventions in regular rituals and routines. Hence, gulf migration is hasn't left any documented revision in their everyday faith forms. Of all the Sunni sections, a well organized cadre culture can be observed in A.P. Faction. In other words, A.P. Faction makes the most of the migration money for managing their movement in the most structured and scientific manner. The group weathered the storm caused by gulf Salafism. In fact, A.P. Faction was untouched by the revision in regular religious understanding. On the other hand, they resisted all the invasive impact Salafi group could introduce to the long-observed system of faith.

Conclusion

The arrival of new religious practises and remittances from the Gulf countries are changing Islamic tradition in Kerala with long-history of Muslim presence. It bears both Positive and negative impact on the life of the Muslims in Kerala. Even though there are some negative impacts, the overall contribution of the gulf relation is very impressive and meaningful for the forward march of a religious minority to the mainstream social life. The traditional and hierarchical nature of the social power structure has been replaced with the emergence of new modernised and democratised individuals and institutions. The Diaspora networks are playing a crucial role in restructuring of the religious institutions and intentions as well. In this social reconstruction, gulf migration not only helped progress wealth but also redefine the social relations in the most rewarding way.

In the beginning of 20th century, all socials sections in Kerala, in a way or another had emerged with some sort of renaissance and wake up call. A miniscule minority played a lead role in these social reform moments. Meanwhile, well lettered social activists in Muslim society had a different road to take. After all, those wake call came from those south districts Muslims were not a fat population. Besides, social reformers like Vakkom Abdul Kader Moulavi had only a little influence in Malabar. The social premises of Malabar Muslims up in arms to resist and repel British colonialism were not ready to receive those wake up calls. The big bragging conservatives faced away all those renewed passion for a change. Following the flight to gulf and financial climb, Muslims in Kerala cleared through all those barriers and blocks stood the way of social upsurge. In brief, the social elevation owing a great deal to gulf migration can be likened to the renaissance and reform led by Sri Narayana Guru among the Hindu community and priests in Christian society.

Bibliography

Books

Abdul Kareem, P (1988): *Education and Economic Development*, New Delhi: Ashish Publications.

Ahmadkutty, E K (1995): "Mujahid Movement and its Role in the Islamic Revival in Kerala" in Asghar Ali Engineer (ed.), *Kerala Muslims: A Historical Perspective*, New Delhi: Ajanta Publications.

Ali, Asghar Engineer (1995): *Kerala Muslims: A Historical Perspective,* New Delhi: Ajanta Publications.

Ali, Hamid (1929): "The Mophlas", in TK Gopal Panicker (ed.) *Malabar and its Folk*, Madrass: GA Nadesan and Company.

Arasaratnam, Sinnappa (1970): *Indians in Malaya and Singapore,* London: Oxford University Press.

Aurora, G.S (1967): *The New Frontiersmen: A Sociological Study of Immigrants in the United Kingdom,* Popular Prakashan: Bombay.

Arango, J. (2004): "Theories of International Migration". in D. Joly (ed.), *International Migration and the New Millennium*. Aldershot: Ashgate.

Amin,Samir (1974) *Modern Migration in Westaern Africa*. Oxford: Oxford University Press.

Barbosa, Durate (1866): *A Description of the Coasts of East Africa and Malabar in the Beginning of the Sixteenth Century*, London: Haklut Society.

Bates, C (2001): *Community, Empire and Migration: South Asians in Diaspora*, Basingstoke: Palgrave.

Birks, J.S, Sinclair, C.A (1980): *International Migration and Development in the Arab Region*, Geneva: ILO.

Birks, J.S. and Sinclair, C.A (1980): *Arab Man Power: The Crisis of Development,* New York: St. Martin's Press.

Boyle, Paul et al (1990): *Exploring Contemporary Migration*, London: Orient Longman.

Brettell, C.B. and Hollifield, J.F.(eds) (2007): *Migration Theory: Talking Across Disciplines*, New York and London: Routledge.

Caplow, Theodore (1975): *The Sociology of Work,* Minneapoly, The University of Minnesotta Press.

Castells, Manuel (1989): *The Informational City: Information Technology, Economic Restructuring and the Urban-Regional Process*, Oxford: Basil Blackwell.

Chant, S. (1992): *Gender and Migration in Developing Countries*, London: Belhaven.

Chakravarti, Nalini Ranjan (1971): *The Indian Minority in Burma: The Rise and Decline of an Immigrant Community,* London: Oxford University Press.

Cohen, Robin eds. (1995): *The Cambridge Survey of World Migration, London:* Cambridge.

Dale, Stephen Frederic (1980): *Moplas of Malabar 1498-1922, Islamic Society on the South Asian Frontier*, London: Cambridge.

Elliot, Emory, Jasmine Payne, Patricia Ploesch (eds.) (2007): *Global Migration Social Change and Cultural Transformation,* London: Palgrave McMillan.

Gardner, Katy and Filippo Osella (1997): *Migration, Modernity, And Social Transformation in South Asia,* New Delhi: Sage Publications.

Gopalan, A.K (1973): *In the Cause of People's Reminiscences*, Bombay: Orient Longman.

Gulati, Leela (1993): *In the Absence of Their Men: The Impact of Male Migration on women*, New Delhi: Sage Publications.

Haas Hein de (2008): Migration and development: A theoretical perspective, Working papers 9, *International migration Institute*, Oxford: University of Oxford.

Hadi Hassan (1928): *A history of Persian Navigation,* London: Routledge.

Iyyer K.V, Krishna (1938): *The Zamorin of Calicut*, Calicut: Novman Printing Bureau.

Jackson, J. A, ed. (1969*): Migration- Sociological Studies*, New York: Cambridge University Press.

Janeen, C.A (1970): *Readings in the Sociolgy of Migration*, London: Pergamon Press.

Johnson, A. G (2007): Blackwell dictionary of sociology, Willey Blackwell, Oxford.

Joseph, K.V (2000): *Migration from Kerala 1920-1960*, Thiruvnanthapuram: Centre for Development Studies.

Joseph, K.V. (1998): *Migration and Economic Development of Kerala,* New Delhi: Mital Publications.

Koya, Mohammed SM (1983): *Mappilas of Malabar: Studies in Social Cultural History,* Thiruvanthapuram: Sandhya Publications.

Kunhali, V (ed.) (2004): *Calicut in History*, Tenhippalam: Publication Division, University of Calicut.

Kunju AP, Ebrahim (1975): *Studies in Medieval Kerala History*, Thiruvanamhapuram: Kerala Historical Society.

Lal, Brij V et al Eds: 2007, The Encyclopedia of Indian Diaspora; Oxford.

Lee, Everett S. (1969): "A Theory of Migration" in J.A Jackson (ed.) *Migration*, London: Cambridge University Press.

Lewis, C.J (1982): *Human Migration: A Geographical perspective*, London and Canberra: Croom Helm.

Mandal, R.B (1981): *Frontiers in Migration Analysis*, New Delhi: Concept Publishing Copmany.

Mangalam, J.J (1968): *Human Migration*, Lexington: University of Kentucky Press.

Mathew, K.S et al (2005): *Migration in South India*, Delhi: Shipra Publications.

Messina M Antony and Gallya Lahav (2006): *The Migration Reader – Exploring Politics and Policies,* London: Lynne Rienner.

Massey, D. J. Arango, G. Hugo, A. Kouaouci, A. Pellegrino, J.E. Taylor,(1998): *Worlds in Motion: Understanding International Migration at the End of the Millenium*, Oxford: Clarendon.

Massey S Douglas et al (2006): "Theories of international Migration: A Review and Appraisal" in Messina M Antony and Gallya Lahav (eds.), The *Migration Reader - Exploring Politics and Policies*, London: Lynne Rienner.

Massey, D. S, Arango, J., Hugo, G., Kouaouci, A., Pellegrino, A., &Taylor, J. E. (1998): *Worlds in Motion. Understanding International Migration at the End of the Millennium*, Oxford: Clarendon Press.

Menon, M. Indu, (1981): *Status of Muslim Women in India: A case study of Kerala,* New Delhi: Uppal Publishing House.

McNeill, W. and Adams, R.S. (1978): *Human Migration: Patterns and Policies*. Bloomington: Indiana University Press.

Miller, Roland E (1976): *Mappila Muslims of Kerala: A study in Islamic Trends*, New Delhi: Orient Longman.

Miller, R.E (1992): *Mappila Muslims Of Kerala; A Study in Islamic trends, Madras*: Orient Longman.

Moulavi, E.K. (1960): "Kerala Muslim Aikya Sangavum Navothanavum" in P.A Said Mohamed (ed.), *Kerala Muslim Directory*, Cochin.

Mowli, Chandra. V (1992): *Bridging the "Gulf": India's Manpower Migrations to West Asia,* New Delhi: Sterling.

Nainar, S. Muhammad Husayn *(1942): Arab Geographers*' Knowledge of Southern India, *Madras*: *University* of *Madras*.

Nair, Gopinathan P.R. (1986): *Asian Migration to the Arab World: Migration from Kerala India*, Thiruvananthapuram: Centre for Development Studies.

Nair, Gopinathan P.R (1981): *Primary Education, Population Growth and Socio-Economic Change: A Comparative Study with Particulalr Reference to Kerala*, New Delhi: Allied Publishers.

Nair, Gopinathan P.R (1988): *Enhancement of Household Capacity in the Post-Migration Phase: A Case Study of India*, Tokyo:The United Nations University.

Nair, Gopinathan P.K (1986): *Asian Migration to the Arab World: Migration from Kerla India*, Trivandrum: Centre for Development Studies.

Nair, Gopinathan (1986): *Asian Migration to the Arab World: Migration from Kerla India*, Trivandrum: Centre for Development Studies.

Oommen, M.A (1971): *Land Reforms and Socio – Economic Change in Kerala: An Introductory Study*, Banglore: The Christian Institute for the Study of Religion and Society.

Panikar, Gopal T K (1995): *Malabar and its Folk, New Delhi,* Madras: Asian Educational Services.

Panicker, K.M (1981): *Malabar and Portuguese*, Trivandrum: S. Viswanathan Printers and Publishers.

Panikkar, K.M (1997): *Malabar and the Portuguese*, New Delhi: Voice of India.

Poonen, T.I (1948): *A survey of the Rise of Dutch Power in India,* Trichinopoly: St Joseph Industrial School Press.

Panicker, K.N (1989): *Against Lord and State: Religion and Peasant Uprisings in Malabar (1826-1921)*, New Delhi: Oxford University Press.

Prakash, B.A (1998): *Indian Migration to the Middle East: Trends, Patterns and Socio-Economic Impact,* Rohtak: Spell bound Publications.

Portes, Alejandro (2008): *Migration and social change*, New Jersey: Princeton University.

Piore J, Michael (1979): *Birds of Passage: Migrant labor in industrial societies*. Cambridge: Cambridge University press.

Portes, A. and Bach, R.L (1985): *Latin Journey: Cuban and Mexican Immigrants in the United States,* Berkeley: University of California Press.

Portes A, Bach R.L (1985): *Latine Journey: Cuban and Mexican immigrants in the United States,* California: University of California Press.

Prema A. Kurien (2003): A Socio-Cultural Perspective on Migration and Economic Development: Middle Eastern Migration from Kerala, India.

Qawasmeh, Engineer Hazem H (2006): Abudhabi: *Population, Economy and Development,* Abudhabi: Environment Agency.

Rajan, Irudaya S and Zachariah, K.C (2008) *Migration and Development: The Kerala Experience,* New Delhi: Danish Publishers.

Rajan, Irudaya S and Marie Percot (2016): *Dynamics of Indian Emigration: Historical and Cultural Perspective*, India: Routlegde.

Rao, Sankar C.N (2005): *Principles of Sociology with an introduction of social thought*, New Delhi: S Chand.

Rao, M.S.A (1957): *Social Change in Malabar*, New Delhi: Popular Book Depot.

Ray D (2003): *Development Economics,* New Delhi: Oxford University Press.

Roland E. Miller (1967): *Mappila Muslims of Kerala- A Study in Islamic Trends,* Bombay Calcutta: Orient Longman.

Samers, M. (2010): *Migration*. London: Routledge.

Sha, Sayed Moideen (1975): *Islam in Kerla,* Trissur: The Muslim Educational Association.

Skeldon Ronald (1997): *Migration and Development: A Global Perspective,* London: Longman.

Saha, Panchanan (1970): *Emigation of Indian Labour (1834 – 1900),* New Delhi: People's Publishing House.

Sekhar, T.V (1997): *Migration and SocialChange,* Jaipur: Rawat Publications.

Shah, Syed Mohidee (1975): *Islam in Kerala*, Trissur:The Muslim Educational Association.

Sinha, V.N.P and Ataullah, Mohammed (1987): *Migration: an Inter Disciplinary Approach*, Delhi: Seemah Publications.

Skeldon, R (1997): *Migration and Development, A Global Perspective,* England: Longman.

Sreedhara Menon A (1967): *A Survey of Kerala History,* Kottayam: National Book Stall.

Tinker, Hugh: A New System of Slavery 1974): *The Export of Indian Labour Overseas 1830-1920*, Bombay: Oxford University Press.

Thomas, D.S. (1941): *Social and Economic Aspects of Swedish Population Movements*, New York: McMillan.

Varghese, T.C (1970): *Agrarian Change and Economic Consequences: Land Tenures in Kerala 1850 – 1960*, Bombay: Allied Publishers.

Viswanathan, S (2001): *Structure and Transformation; Theory and Society in India*, New Delhi: Oxford University Press.

Wallerstein, I (1979): *The Capitalist World Economy*. Cambridge: Cambridge University Press.

Willox, Walter F (1969): *International Migration*, New York: Gorden Reach Publications.

Zachariah, K.C, Rajan S Irudaya (2012): *Kerala's Gulf Connection, 1998-2011: Economic and Social Impact of Migration,* New Delhi: Orient BlackSwan.

Zachariah, K.C and Irudaya Rajan S (1997): *Kerala's Demographic Transition, Determinants and consequences*, New Delhi: Sage.

Zachariah, K.C and Irudaya Rajan S (2012): Inflexion in Kerlas Gulf Connection: *Report on Kerala Migration Survey,* Thiruvananthapuram: Centre for Development Studies.

Zachariah, K.C and Irudaya Rajan S (2007): "Migration Remittences and Employment: Short term trends and long term implications,*Working paper 385*, Thiruvananthapuram: Centre for Development Studies.

Zachariah, K.C and Irudaya Rajan, S, eds (1997): *Kerala's Demographic Transition: Determinants and Consequences*, New Delhi: Sage Publications.

Zachariah, K.C et al (2003): *Dynamics of Migration in Kerala: Dimensions, Differentials and Consequences*, New Delhi: Orient Longman.

Journal Articles

Abdurahman, O (1964): "Jamaethe Islami in Kerala" (Mal),*Prabodhanam* special issue, Kozhikode: Islamic Publishing House.

Agesa, Richard U (2001): "Migration and the Urban to Rural Earning Difference: A Sample Section Approach",*Economic Development and Cultural Change*, 49(4):847-865.

Boyd, M (1989): "Family and personal networks in migration", *International Migration Review*, 23(3): 638-70.

Boyd, M. and Nowak, J. (2012): "Social Networks and International Migration", in Martiniello,M. and Rath, J. (eds.),*An Introduction toInternational Migration Studies*, Amsterdam: Amsterdam University Press.

Castles, S. (2010): "Understanding Global Migration: A Social Transformation Perspective",*Journal of Ethnic and Migration Studies*, 36(10): 1565-1586.

Chandavarkar, Anand G (1980): "Use of Migrants' Remittances in Labour Exporting Countries", *Finance and Development*, 17(2), June 1980: 36-39.

Damayanthi, U.T (1995): "Declining Importance of Land in Generating Rural Employment in Kerala", *Manpower Journal*, 31(2), July – September: 47-51.

Desai, A.R (1987): "Trends of Change in Indian Society since Independence", *Economic and Political Weekly*, 24(33)August 19.

Gulati, Leela (1997): "Coping with Male Migration", *Economic and Political Weekly* 22(44), October 31:41-46.

Gulati, Leela (1998): "Migration and Social Change in Kerala", *Indian International Centre Quarterly*, 22(03), Mansoon 1998:191-202.

Haas, Hein De.(2006) "Migration, Remittances and Regional development in Southern Morocco." *Geoforum* 37: 565-580.

Haas, Hein De, (2009): "Mobility and Human Development", working Paper 14, *International Migration Institute*, University of Oxford.

Ilahiane, H. (2001): "The social mobility of the Haratine and the re-working of Bourdieu's Habitus on the Saharan frontier, Morocco." *American Anthropologist* 103: 380-394.

Jetley, S. (1987): "Impact of Male Migration on Rural Females", *Economic and Political Weekly*, 22(44): 47-53.

Jayawardena, Chandra (1968): "Migration and Social Change: A Survey of Indian Communities Overseas" *Geographical Review*, American Geographical Society, 58 (3): 426-449.

Kutty, Ahmed E.K (1978): "Islam and Social Reform Movements in Kerala", *Journal of Kerala Studies*, V(4), December, 439-451.

Klooster, D.J. (2005): "Producing social nature in the Mexican countryside." *Cultural Geographies* 12: 321-344.

Levitt, Peggy (1998): "Social Remittances: Migration Driven Local-Level Forms of Cultural Diffusion", *International Migration Review* 32: 926-948.

Lee, E.S. (1966): "A Theory of Migration", *Demography*, 3(1): 47-57.

Mathew, ET and PR Gopinathan Nair:(1978), "Socio-Economic Charactoristics of Emigrants and Emigrants household: A study of Two Villages in Kerla", *Economic and Political Weekly*, 13(28), July 15: 1141-1153.

Massey, Taylor, J.E. (1993): "Theories of international migration: review and appraisal". *Population and Development Review* 19: 431–466.

Massey, Douglas et al(1993): "Theories of International Migration: A Review and Appraisal" *Population and Development Review* 19(3): 431-466.

Massy, Douglas (1989): "The settlement process among Mexican Migrants to the United States" *American Sociological Review*, 51: 670-685.

Massey, D.S, (1990): "Social Structure, Household Strategies and the Cumulative Cuasation of Migration", *Population Index*, 56 (1): 3-26.

Muhammed N.P(2002): "Kerla Muslimkalude Samskarika Paschathalam" (ML) *Riyad KMCC Sovenier*: Riyadh.

Mutersbaugh, T. (2002): "Migration, common property, and communal labor: cultural politics and agency in a Mexican village." *Political Geography* 21: 473-494.

Osella, Filippo and Caroline Osella (2000): "Migration, Money and Masculinity in Kerala", *The Journal of the Royal Anthropological institute*, 6(1), March: 119.

Percot, Marie and Rajan S, Irudaya (2007): "Female Emigration from India: Case Study of Nurses", *Economic and Political Weekly*, Volume 42 (4): 318-325.

Prakash, B. A. (1998) "Gulf Migration and Its Economic Impact: The Kerala Experience" *Economic and Political Weekly*, 33 (50): 3209-3213.

Prakash, B. A,(1978): "Impact of Foreign Remittances: A Case Study of Chavakkad Village", *Economic and Political Weekly*, XIII (27), July 8: 1107-1111.

Prakash, B. A. (1998): Gulf Migration and Its Economic Impact: The Kerala Experience, *Economic and Political Weekly*, 33(50).

Psuda, Teakyuki (1995) "The Motivation to Migrate: The Ethnic and Socio Cultural Constitutions of the Japanese Brazilian return Migration System", *Economic Development and Cultural Change*, 48(1) Chicago.

Radhakrishnan and Ibrahim (1981): "Emigration inward remittances and Economic Development: with particular reference to the emigration from Kerala to the Persian Gulf Countries", *Manpower Journal*, 13(4): New Delhi.

Rajan, Irudaya S and Zachariah, K.C (2001): "Gender Dimensions of Migration in Kerala: Macro and Micro Evidence", *Asia Pacific Population Journal*, 16 (3):47-70.

Ravenstein E.G(1885): "The Laws of Migration". *Journal of the Royal Statistical Society* 48(2):167-227.

Taylor, M. J, Moran-Taylor, and D. R. Ruiz (2006): "Land, ethnic, and gender change; Transnational migration and its effects on Guatemalan lives and landscapes." *Geoforum* 37:41-61.

Tilly, C. and Brown C, H, (1967): "On Uprooting, Kinship and Urban Unemployment in Less developed Countries", *The American Economic Review*, LIX (1): 138-148.

Van Hear, Nicholas (2010): "Theories of Migration and Social Change", *Journal of Ethnic and Migration Studies*, 36 (10): 1531- 1536 .

Vijayan M.N (2004) "Nammude Rosham GulfilNinnu Kondu Vannathalla", *Chandrika Weekly* Kozhikode: 28 (3).

Wood, Charles H (1981): "Equilibrium and Historical Structural Perspectives on Migration", *International Migration Review*, 16(2), Summer 1982: 298-319.

Zachariah, K.C and Rajan, Irudaya S. (2004): "Gulf Emigration of Women in Kerala" *Samyukta, A Journal of Women's Studies,* IV(2): 41-52.

Zachariah, K.C and Rajan, Irudaya. (2001) "Migration Mosaic in Kerala; Trends and Determinants" *Demography India*, 30 (1):137-165.

Zachariah, K.C, E.T. Mathew and S.Irudaya Rajan, "Social,Economic and Demographic Consequences of Migration on Kerala" *International Migration*, 39(2): 43-71.

Zachariah, K.C, E.T. Mathew and S.Irudaya Rajan, "Impact of Migration on Kerala's Economy and Society" *InternationalMigration*, 39 (1): 63-88.

Zachariah, K.C and Rajan S, Irudaya (2004): "Gulf Emigration of Women in Kerala" *Samyukta, A Journal of Women's Studies,* IV(2): 41-52.

Zachariah, K.C and Rajan, Irudaya. (2001) "Migration Mosaic in Kerala; Trends and Determinants" *Demography India*, 30 (1): 137-165.

Books - Malayalam

Benyamin (2017): *Kudiyettam,* Kottayam: DC Books.

Ganesh, K N (1990) *Keralathinte Innalekal,* Trivandrum: Department of Cultural Publications.

Kutty, Ahmad E K (2010): Kerala Muslim Navothanam: Vimarsanangalum Vasthuthakalaum, Kozhikode: Yuvatha Book House.

Pokker, P K (2012): *Swathwa Rashtreeyam,* Calicut: Progress.

Sullamai, MI Muhammadali (2002): *Gulf Salafisavum Mujahid Prasthanavum*, Malappuram: Al-Furqan Publications.

Journal Articles – Malayalam

Abdul Azees, T(1995): "Kerala Muslimkalude Charithra Paschathalam", *Chandrika Weekly*, 9 September.

Abdulla, T (1998): "Muslimkal Kooduthal Pinnokkavasthayilekku", *Chandrika Weekly*, 1 May.

Abdul Gafoor, P.K (1967): "MES Purogathiyil Ninnu Purogathiyilekku", *Kozhikode District MES Souvenir* .

Aboo, K.K (2000): "Oru Thirichu Varavinte Katha", *Kuwait Kerala Muslim Culturala Centre Relief Fund souvenir*.

Bava, Faisal (2006): "Gulf Malayaliyude Rashtriya Mukham", *Sastragathi Monthly*,

Bhaskar, B.R.P (2007): "Thudarchayayi Parachayappedunna Aasuthranam", *Social Review Monthly*, January.

Gafoor, Fazal (2016): "Nammal Chuvadu Vacha 60 Varshangal", *Shabab Weekly* Nov 4: 4-14.

Hassan, Sidhiq (1998): "Jamathe Islami Keralathil", *Prabodhanan Weeklly*, April: 138.

Kabeer, M (2007): "Samoohika Parishkaranavum Muslimkalum", *Social Review Monthly*, January.

Hameed, Chennamangallor (1998): "Muslimkalude Vidhyabhyasa Pinnokkavastha: Karanavum Prathividhiyum", *Chandrika Weekly*, 8 August.

Ibrahim, P (2004): "Kudiyethathinte Sishtam", *Chandrika Weekly*, 28 August.

Joseph, K.V (1984): "Gulf Panavum Karshika Vethanavum", *Mathrubhumi Weekly, 14* February.

Koya, Mohammed C.H (1966): 'Muslim Samudayam Abhimukekarikkunna Prasnangal', Kannur District Muslim Educational Association Souvenir.

Koya, Mohammed SM (1998): "Kerala Muslimkal Udaya Vikasangal", *Farook College Golden Jubilee Souvenier.*

Kunhukkuttan, Madambu (1980): 'Ezham Kadalinu Akkareyullavarodu', *Abudhabi Malayali Samajam Souvenir.*

Kunju, Ibrahim A.P (1998): "Kerala Muslimkal Avirbhavavum Vyapanavum", *Farook College Golden Jubilee Souvenier*.

Mohammed Ali, K.T (1998): "Kerala Muslimkal Arabian Verukal", *Farook College Golden Jubilee Souvenier*.

Mohammed, A.M (2007): "Keralthinu Veliyile Keralam: Gulf", *Madyamam Annual.*

Mohammed, C.A (1967): "Vidhyabhyasa Rangathe Muslim Pinnokkavastha", *Kozhikode Distict MES Souvenir.*

Mohammed, Habeeb P.S (1967): "Muslimkalude Vidhyabhyasa Purogathi", *Kozhikode Distict MES Souvenir.*

Mohammed, Hafis N.P (1998): "Kerala Muslimkal Saviseshathakalude Samooham", *Farook College Golden Jubilee Souvenier.*

Mohammed, Hafiz N.P (2001): "Vibhava Seshi Vikasathinte Parinamangal", *Thelicham Varshikappatippu.*

Mohammed, Karuvalli (1998): "Arabi Islamika Vidhyabhyasam Keralathil", *Farook College Fortieth Anniversary Souvenier.*

Mathew, Kosi P (2007): "Karshika Prasnavum Vikasana Prasnangalum", *Social Review Monthly.*

Narayanan, M.G.S (1998): "Kerala Muslimkal Arabi Likhithagalile Prakasam", *Farook College Golden Jubilee Souvenir.*

Narayanan, Manajakkulam (2007): "Keralappiraviyude Anpatham Varshikavum Pravasikalude Pankum", *Pravasam 2007, Kerala Pravasi Sangam Souvenir.*

Nirmal Kumar, K.P (2004): "Vattunna Viyarppinteyum Vilayatha Nanyathinteyum Kalam", *Mathrubhumi Weekly*, 08 August.

Panicker, K.N (2008): "Saamoohika Mattathinte Puthiya Vegangal", *Madyamam Weekly Onappathippu.*

Rahman, U.P.A Kilinakkode (2006): "Malappurathinte Varthamanam Ethra Bhayanakam", *Thelicham Monthly*, February.

Rafeeq, Parambath (2001): "Gulfum Kazhiyunnu, Eni Enthu", *Chandrika Weekly*, 6 November.

Rahmatullah, K.P.O (1990): "Gulf Prathisandiyum Malayaliyude Bhaviyum", Kalakaumudi Weekly, 29 September.

Rajasekharan, P.K (1991): "Parasyangalude Saamoohya Prasakthi", *Mathrubhumi Weekly*, 20 January.

Sakkariya (2007): "Chila Dubai Viseshangal", *Kala Kaumudi Weekly*, 18 November.

Shihabudheen, Poithumkadavu (2004): "Driverum Cheriyoru Pilottalle Sir", *Mathrubhumi Weekly*, 14 June.

Sihabudheen Poithumkadavu (2008): "Drivarum Cheriyoru Pailattalle saar", *Mathrubhoomi Weekly*, Kozhikode June (8-14).

Sreedharan, K (2006): "Anpathu Varshathe Kerala Vikasananubhavangal Tharunnathenth", *Mathrubhumi Weekly*, 23 December.

Suresh, P (2006): "Keraleeyar Puram Nadukalil Paniyedukkumbol Samhavikkunnath", *Sasthrgathi Monthly*, Kozhikode, November 7: 18-23.

Varrier, Raghava M.R (1998): "Kerala Muslimkal Samskarika Vikiranathinte Prakasanam", *Farook College Golden Jubilee Souvenier.*

Vazhakkad, Sadarudhin (2016): "Dhammaj Dhara Akshara Salafisathinte Azhiyakkurukkukal", *Prabodhanam Weekly*, July 22: 39.

Vijayan, M.N (2004): "Nammude Rosham Gulfil Ninnu Kondu Vannathalla", *Chandrika Weekly*, 28 August.

News Paper Articles - Malayalam

Abdulla, Bevinja (2008): "Pravasi Nilavili Nilakkunnilla", *Mathrubhumi Daily*, 03 April.

Abdulla, K (1988): "Gulf Swapnangale Vida", *Mathrubhumi Daily*, 18 February.

Abdullakkoya, P.V (1987): "Gulfil Ninnu Madangunnavarkku Vyavasaya Soukaryangal Enthokke?", *Mathrubhumi Daily*, 6 January.

Chandran, Sarath C (2004): "Videsathu Parkkunna Midukkan Malayali", *Malayala Manorama Daily*, 27 August.

Gangadaran, T.P (1999): "Namukku Parkkan Concrete Kadukal", *Mathrubhumi Daily*, 29 October.

Ibraheem, Kottakkal (1998): "Athuralayangalil Arogyakkachavadam", *Madhyamam Daily*, 15 December.

Joseph K.V (2000): "Gulf Panam Keralthinte Vikasanathinu Uthakanam", *Malayala Manorama Daily*, 15 August.

Kumar, Vijaya K.P (2006): "Gulf Swapnam Asthamayathinte Thudakkam", *Thejas Daily*, 01-07 September .

Madhu, Vechoochira (1988): "Gulf Swapnangale Vida", *Mathrubhumi Daily*, 9 – 11 February .

Mohammed, Kakkad (2008): "Gulf Malayalikalum Perukunna Kutta Krithyanglum", *Chandrika Daily*, 29 March.

Nair, Sekharan G (1987): "Akkarappacha", *Mathrubhumi Daily*, 12 – 25 January.

Nisar, Olavanna (2000): "Chiraku Karinha Swapnangalumayi Madangiyavar', *Chandrika Daily*, 04 - 07 November.

Pillai, Ramachandran R (1985): "Gulf Jeevitham: Sambathika Samoohika Prasnangal", *Mathrubhumi Daily*, 11 September.

Raj, Biju N.S (2000): "Nilakkunna Ennappanam Nilavidunna Keralam", *Mathrubhumi Daily*, 15 May.

Razak, Orumanayoor (2001): "Pravasi Prasnam", *Chandrika Daily*, 06 August.

Surendran, M.P (1988): "Gulf Swapnangale Vida", *Mathrubhumi Daily*, 20 February.

Reports and Working Papers

Zacharia, K.C et al (1999): Impacts of Migration on Kerala's Economy and Society, *Working paper No.297*, Trivandrum: Centre for Development Studies.

Hass, Hein De (2010): "Migration transitions: a theoretical and empirical inquiry into the developmental drivers of international migration", *Internatioanal Migraton Institute, Working Paper 24*, London: University of Oxford.

Collinson, S (2009): "The Political Economy of Migration Processes: An Agenda for Migration Research and Analysis", *International Migration Institute, IMI Working Paper 12,* University of Oxford:

Rajan, S Irudaya and Zachariah, K.C (2005): "Unemployment in Kerala at the Turn of the Century:Insights from CDS Gulf Migration Studies" *Working Paper No. 374.* Thiruvananthapuram. Centre for Development Studies.

De Haan, Arjan (2000): "Migrants, Livelihoods, and Rigths: The relevance of Migration in Development Policies", *Social Development Department Working Paper, 4,* DFID.

Rajan, S Irudaya and U S Mishra (2007) "Managing Migration in the Philippines: Lessons for India", CDS *working Paper 393,* Thiruvananthapuram: Centre for Development Studies.

Irudaya Rajan, S and Prabhat Kumar (2007): "International Migration From India In The Last Two Centuries" *Paper presented at the National Seminar on Indian Economy: Historical Roots and Contemporary Development Experience,* Thiruvananthapuram, Centre for Development Studies .

Gulati I.S, and A. Mody (1983) "Remittances of Indian migrants to the Middle East: An assessment with special reference to migrants from Kerala state", *Working Paper 182.* Trivandrum: Centre for Development Studies.

Zachariah, Mathew, Rajan (1999) "Impact of migration on Kerala's economy and society", *Working Paper 297,* Trivandrum, Centre for Development Studies.

Gulati and Mody (1983) "Remittances of Indian migrants to the Middle East: An assessment with special reference to migrants from Kerala state", *Working Paper 182,*, Trivandrum, Centre for Development Studies.

Zachariah, K.C., E. T. Mathew, and S. I. Rajan 1999 "Impact of migration on Kerala's economy and society", Working Paper 297, Centre for Development Studies, Trivandrum, Kerala.

Psuda,Teakyuki (1995): The Motivation to Migrate: The Ethnic and Socio Cultural Constitutions of the Japanese Brazilian return Migration System, *Economic Development and Cultural Change*, Vol 48(1) Chickago.

Zacharia, K.C et al (1999): Impacts of Migration on Kerala's Economy and Society, Working paper No. 297 CDS).

Zacharia, K.C et al (1999): Impacts of Migration on Kerala's Economy and Society, Working paper No.297 CDS) pp. 27.

Reports

Government of Kerala/Department of Economics and Statistics (1987), *Report of the Survey on the Utilisation of Gulf Remittances in Kerala,* Trivandrum: Government of Kerala.

NORKA (2013), Pravasi Malayali Census Report, Govt. of Kerala.

Sachaar Committee Report, (2006): Social, Economic and Educational Status of the Muslim Community of India, Prime Minister's High Level Committee, Government of India.

The Commerce Research Bureau, (1978):"Emigration and Inward Remittances and Economic Growth of Kerala, Report of a Survey of Government of India, Bombay.

Government of India/Ministry of Labour (2000), *Annual Report - 1999-2000*, New Delhi: Government of India.

Index